Grades 9–12

Grammar Notebook
for
Sentence Structure

Understanding the Why's and How's of American English Grammar

Janelle Diller

These popular teacher resources and activity books are available from
ECS Learning Systems, Inc., and Novel Units, Inc.

ECS9676	Destinations	Grades 5-9
NU783XRH	Graphic Organizer Collection	Grades 3-12
ECS9501	Hemingway for Teachers	Grades 9-12
ECS9609	Inkblots	Grades 6-12
ECS0484	Not More Writing?!	Grades 9-12
ECS9633	Odysseys	Grades 5-9
ECS948X	Quick Thinking	Grades 7-12
ECS9706	Springboards for Reading	Grades 7-12
ECS0549	Structures for Reading, Writing, Thinking Book 1	Grades 4-9
ECS0557	Structures for Reading, Writing, Thinking Book 2	Grades 4-9
ECS0565	Structures for Reading, Writing, Thinking Book 3	Grades 4-9
ECS0573	Structures for Reading, Writing, Thinking Book 4	Grades 4-9
NU5958RH	Tackling Literary Terms	Grades 9-12
ECS9439	Tactics to Tackle Thinking	Grades 7-12
ECS9668	Voyages	Grades 5-9
ECS9080	Writing Warm-Ups	Grades 7-12
ECS9463	Writing Warm-Ups Two	Grades 7-12

To order, or for a complete catalog, write:

ECS Learning Systems, Inc.
P.O. Box 791439
San Antonio, Texas 78279-1439

Web site: www.educyberstor.com
or contact your local school supply store.

Editor: Shirley J. Durst
Cover Design and Page Layout: Anh N. Le

ISBN 1-57022-238-X

Author's Note

I have a confession to make: I love grammar. Consequently, in most people's eyes, this makes me a little peculiar (I prefer the term "slightly eccentric," but I usually don't get to choose). If I have to name any single reason for why grammar fascinates me, it's because long ago I learned to enjoy the quirkiness of language. And English abounds in quirkiness. For instance, it's perfectly acceptable to ask: "I'm going with you, aren't I?" or "I'm going with you, am I not?" On the other hand, it's perfectly *unacceptable* to ask, "I'm going with you, are I not?" or "I'm going with you, amn't I?"

Infinitives present even more language quirkiness. In Latin (one of the root languages of English), infinitives literally cannot be "split" because in that language the infinitive form of a verb is a single word. As a result, some English language grammarians insist that infinitives should never be split. For example, using the infinitive *to double*, I would ordinarily say, "He plans *to more than double* his income by August." To keep from splitting the infinitive, I apparently *should* say, "He plans *more than to double* his income" or "He plans *to double more than* his income."

It is my belief that the joy felt in the exploration of a language is proportionate to how that language is eventually used. Consider the following analogy: Recently, I went to a Colorado Nuggets game with a young basketball fanatic friend of mine. Having a rudimentary understanding of how the game is played (ten people, one ball, big court, little basket), I enjoyed myself. My friend, however, was in ecstasy. He knew the statistics, strategies, potentials—every possible tidbit about each player and the overall game. I know that if I attended every game of the season with him, his knowledge would give me far greater enthusiasm for the sport.

The **Grammar Notebook** series is designed to give your students this kind of "courtside enthusiasm" for English grammar. The idea is for learners to start listening and observing, thinking and using the structure and rules of English in ways that they previously have not. Ultimately, as they begin to understand the "why's" of English grammar, they will be able to do the "how's." Whether they're trying to absorb a new grammar rule or change the way they speak and write, this is the best way to learn!

Janelle Diller

Janelle Diller

　　　　ECS Learning Systems, Inc.　　　　The Grammar Notebook

About the Author

Janelle Diller has taught high school, college, and workplace English, as well as directed the customized training division at Pikes Peak Community College (PPCC) in Colorado Springs, Colorado. Ms. Diller has developed curricula for workplace education which have been shared and adopted nationally. She has made presentations nationally and internationally on curriculum development and workplace education issues. Ms. Diller has also co-authored, with her husband, two books and a video for the construction industry. Her first novel, *For the Love of Gold* (Royal Fireworks Press) was selected as a Kansas State Reading Council choice in 1998-99.

Ms. Diller lives in Colorado Springs with her husband and two sons, who are all pleasantly tolerant of her love of grammar.

Table of Contents

Author's Note

About the Author

ix   **Introduction**

      Beyond Drills and Prewritten Exercises
      Learning from Student Writing
      What's Inside
      Breaking the Traditional Teaching Mold
      Teaching What You Know
      Learning Styles
      Conclusion

xiii   **Before You Begin (For Students)...**

      Why Study Sentence Structure?
      Grammar Resources

Sentence Structure

2   **Subjects**

      Simple Subjects
      Complete Subjects
      Compound Subjects
      Exceptions: Questions, Expletive Sentences, and Imperative
            (Command) Sentences

5   **It's Your Turn:** Simple Subjects and Complete Subjects

6   **Predicates**

      Simple Predicates
      Complete Predicates
      Compound Predicates

7   **It's Your Turn:** Complete Subjects and Complete Predicates

9   **Subject/Verb Agreement**

Singular and Plural Subjects
Either…or, neither…nor
Subject Separated from the Verb
Verb before the Subject
Collective Nouns

12   **It's Your Turn:** Subject/Verb Agreement

14   **Review:** What Have You Learned So Far?

15   **Language Play:** English as the Official Language

16   **Clauses**

Independent Clauses
Dependent Clauses
Noun, Adjective, and Adverb Clauses

18   **It's Your Turn:** Clauses

Sentence Fragments

20   **It's Your Turn:** Sentence Fragments

21   **Phrases**

Prepositional Phrases
Gerund Phrases
Participle Phrases
Infinitive Phrases

23   **It's Your Turn:** Phrases

The Grammar Notebook   ECS Learning Systems, Inc.

Sentence Structures A, B, C, D, and E

25   **Chart:** Traditional/*Grammar Notebook* Sentence Structure
Classification

26   **Sentence Structure A**

Features and Examples
What to Watch Out For: Unnecessary Commas

28   **It's Your Turn:** Sentence Structure A

29   **Sentence Structure B**

Features and Examples
What to Watch Out For: Run-on Sentences, Comma Splices,
Using Semicolons, Using Colons

33   **It's Your Turn:** Sentence Structures A and B

35   **Sentence Structure C**

Features and Examples
What to Watch Out For: Punctuation Between Clauses,
Using *That*, *So,* and *So that*

37   **It's Your Turn:** Sentences Structures A, B, and C

38   **Sentence Structure D**

Features and Examples
What to Watch Out For: Comma Omissions

40   **It's Your Turn:** Sentence Structures A, B, C, and D

41   **Sentence Structure E**

Features and Examples
What to Watch Out For: Punctuating Restrictive and
Nonrestrictive Clauses

44   It's Your Turn: Sentence Structures A, B, C, D, and E

45   Chart: Summary Sheet: A, B, C, D, and E Structure Sentences

46   It's Your Turn: More Sentence Structures A, B, C, D, and E

47   Review: What Have You Learned So Far?

48   Tips for Stronger Sentences

Misplaced and Dangling Modifiers

51   It's Your Turn: Misplaced and Dangling Modifiers

Active and Passive Voice

54   Chart: Active and Passive Voice

55   It's Your Turn: Active and Passive Voice

Parallel Sentence Structure

57   It's Your Turn: Reading for Parallel Sentence Structure

60   Review: What Have You Learned So Far?

61   Appendix

What's Your Learning Style?
Teaching What You Know
The TRUSS System
The Gunning Fog Index
More Tips for Stronger Sentences
New Word List Form
Usage Errors Form

74   Answer Key

The Grammar Notebook   ECS Learning Systems, Inc.

Introduction

Beyond Drills and Prewritten Exercises

Imagine a set of jigsaw puzzles. Although the pictures on the backs of the puzzle pieces vary significantly, each time you put the puzzles together, it gets easier. Eventually you don't have to pay as much attention to the puzzle shapes because you recognize which pieces fit together. As a result, you can spend more time enjoying the pictures, rather then laboring to put the puzzle pieces together.

Building strong, clear structures is a little like putting a puzzle together. Clauses, phrases, and conjunctions represent the puzzle pieces and their various shapes. Words combined in particular ways create a picture. With practice, sentence structure rules become more automatic, allowing the writer to concentrate on the content of the writing, rather than the mechanics.

Although standard rules and explanations for writing clearer sentences are included, the focus of the **Grammar Notebook** series is shifted away from customary drills and toward helping learners develop a better understanding of the "why's" and "how's" of grammar. The intent is to build thinking skills around why we follow certain language conventions and to make the rules easier to learn and use.

Learning from Student Writing

As much as possible, grammar should be taught and practiced within the context of students' own writing. This presents a challenge for the instructor. When grammar is taught with textbook or prewritten exercises, students may learn to recognize the concepts and still not be able to transfer what they've learned to their own writing. On the other hand, when teachers use only student work, instruction can seem disorganized and fragmented, with every aspect of grammar touched on but no one explained completely.

The best approach is a combination of the two. In addition to prewritten exercises, students should always practice writing their own examples. They should also look for correct or incorrect examples in their everyday writing. To encourage this process, each book in the **Grammar Notebook** series follows a simple teaching progression:

1. Explain each new concept to students, answering questions and giving lots of examples. (Use the chalkboard or transparencies to make points and to show example sentences.)

ECS Learning Systems, Inc. The Grammar Notebook

2. Work through the sample sentences in each section with students. This step gives you a window to what they understand and what they do not, as well as an opportunity to explain a concept from a new angle, if necessary.

3. Guide students in practicing the concepts by themselves, in pairs, or in groups. As an optional activity, have them examine their own work in other subject areas for examples of how they've correctly or incorrectly used a new concept. (To avoid hours of tedious grading, students can review each other's work in small groups, using the teacher for reference only.)

4. Encourage students to become aware of interesting uses of language. Have them learn and identify a minimum of three new words each week, describing how they learned each new word and how and when they used it (see Appendix, page 71).

5. Encourage students to listen and read for usage errors on TV, radio, or in print. Have them identify what the correct usage should have been and whether the usage error was intentional. Follow up by having them describe the impact an intentional usage error may have had on the reader or listener (see Appendix, page 73).

What's Inside

To support the learning process described above, **Grammar Notebook** features the following:

- explanations of grammatical terms and/or rules

- examples that illustrate the terms and/or rules

- tips for remembering correct usage

- points for class or group discussion

- practice sentences for identifying correct usage

- exercises for practicing correct usage with students' own sentences

- a structure for student-led teaching of concepts

- a review of how students are applying what they've learned

- an opportunity for students to document what they have learned so far and to think about what they still want to learn

The Grammar Notebook ECS Learning Systems, Inc.

Finally, scattered throughout the text are sections entitled "Language Play." These sections make excellent discussion or essay starters. Each Language Play describes the lively and ever-changing nature of English and features opportunities for greater exploration of how our language is changing. The intent here is to awaken learners to the realization that not only does English continuously change, but that each of us is an active contributor to the ongoing metamorphosis.

Breaking the Traditional Teaching Mold

Education and sports—analogies abound.

Think for a few minutes of teachers and students in a traditional classroom situation as the pitcher and catcher on a baseball team. They're both on the same team and have common goals. The pitcher's purpose is to throw the ball; the catcher's is to catch it. As the ball flies through the air, somewhere between the pitcher and the catcher the responsibility shifts. The catcher is not responsible for the ball while it's still in the pitcher's hands. By the same token, the pitcher—even when the ball is poorly thrown—is not responsible for the ball once it is in the catcher's territory.

So it is in the traditional classroom. The teacher delivers information and students receive it. Once the teacher has "pitched" the information, it's up to the student to "catch" it. Somewhere in this process the responsibility shifts from teacher to student. Even if the information is poorly taught, the student is still responsible for knowing it.

A better way to learn is for both teacher and student to take responsibility during the entire process. The earlier learners actively participate in the learning process, the more likely it is that they will truly understand the information and be able to apply it to something similar but not necessarily directly related. Likewise, the teacher's responsibility should not end as soon as the information has been delivered. If teachers go beyond traditional lines and expectations, students will be far more likely to understand, and, in the process, become better learners in general.

Teaching What You Know

Clearly, one of the most effective ways to learn something is to teach it. Schedule times for students to teach each other or reinforce concepts they're learning. Try a mix of the following teaching methods:

- Planned, but informal, lessons where students work in groups of two or three

- Spontaneous, five-minute lessons during class where students pair up and improve their understanding about something you've covered that day

To reduce student anxiety, students should begin with informal teaching sessions (see Appendix, page 63). At least initially, don't grade on the quality of the lesson. As students' ability to explain concepts increases, offer them opportunities to share their spontaneous or informal lessons with the rest of the class.

Learning Styles

The **Grammar Notebook** series makes an effort to combine all three learning styles (auditory, visual, and kinesthetic) in both structured and nonstructured ways. As a teacher, you'll address both auditory and visual learning needs. The many practice and writing exercises included in **Grammar Notebook** are excellent for kinesthetic learning. These three learning styles are again reinforced as students are encouraged to listen to how others are using grammar, watch for usages as they read, and teach others what they are learning (see Appendix, page 62).

Conclusion

Most of all, remember to have fun with the subject. The rich history of English has created a language resonating with variety, texture, and color. If you, the teacher, can inspire students to grasp this, the rest will easily follow.

Before You Begin (For Students)...

Why Study Sentence Structure?

Without even being aware of it, people make subtle—and sometimes not so subtle—value judgments about others based on their language skills. If a person has a large vocabulary and follows standard rules, he or she is treated differently than someone whose vocabulary is limited or who ignores even basic grammar rules. As a result, people whose language skills aren't as polished or sophisticated as they should be are often passed over for job promotions—even when they have all the other necessary qualifications. This happens whether or not writing or oral skills are required to do the job well.

1. Think of a time when someone judged you either positively or negatively because of your grammar. Or think of a time when you judged someone favorably or unfavorably because of his or her grammar. Describe what happened and what you learned from the experience. Did the experience change you in any way?

2. What changes would you like to make in your writing?

3. On a separate sheet of paper, brainstorm every writing term you can think of. Use more pages if necessary. Go back and put a check mark in front of the ones you understand how to use already.

4. List the questions you have about grammar. What grammar skills would you like to learn? As you learn more about grammar, return to these pages to add new terms and skills and to check off the ones you have mastered.

Grammar Resources

List the resources you have for learning about grammar (books, people, places). Return to this list and add other helpful resources as you find them.

BOOKS

_____   _____

_____   _____

_____   _____

_____   _____

_____   _____

PEOPLE

_____   _____

_____   _____

_____   _____

_____   _____

_____   _____

PLACES

_____   _____

_____   _____

_____   _____

_____   _____

_____   _____

The Grammar Notebook   ECS Learning Systems, Inc.

Sentence Structure

Subjects

Subjects and **predicates** are the building blocks of sentences. The **subject** tells *who* or *what* a sentence is about. The **predicate** tells what a subject is *doing* or *being*. Without both a subject and a predicate, a sentence is not a sentence.

Simple Subjects

The **simple subject** is the noun or pronoun the sentence is about. Simple subjects—

- almost always come early in the sentence

- usually come before the verb

- are never in a prepositional phrase

■ Tip

To find the simple subject, ask who or what the sentence is about, or ask who or what is doing something in the sentence.

1) The neighbors' ***dogs*** are fighting again.
   (Who is fighting? The dogs are fighting, not the neighbors.)

2) ***It*** doesn't matter who wins.
   (What doesn't matter? It doesn't matter.)

3) The ***car*** in the middle lane blew a tire.
   (What blew a tire? The car blew a tire, not the middle lane.)

The Grammar Notebook   ECS Learning Systems, Inc.

Complete Subjects

The **complete subject** includes the simple subject and all the words that describe it. The complete subject may either be one word or several words:

    1) *The neighbors' dogs* are fighting again.

    2) *It* doesn't matter who wins.

    3) *The car in the middle lane* blew a tire.

Subjects may be singular or plural:

    Singular (one subject): A *student* is expected to study hard.
                             The apple *tree* blooms every year.

    Plural (more than one subject): *Students* are expected to study hard.
                                      Apple *trees* bloom every year.

Compound Subjects

Compound subjects (two or more subjects) are joined by the coordinating conjunctions *and*, *or*, *but*, or *nor*. No comma is placed between the subjects unless three or more subjects are used.

    1) **The soccer team** and **the lacrosse team** are raising money for new uniforms. (two subjects)

    2) **The cheerleaders**, **pep club**, and **marching band** are helping. (three subjects)

Exceptions: Questions, Expletive Sentences, and Imperative (Command) Sentences

Sometimes the subject does not come before the verb (predicate), as in **questions** and in **expletive** and **imperative (command) sentences**.

Questions

For **questions**, find the subject by turning the question into a statement:

    1) What impact did television have on the external history of English?
       Television did have an impact on the external history of English.

    2) How did the game end?
       The *game* did end.

         ECS Learning Systems, Inc.   The Grammar Notebook

Expletive Sentences

For **expletive sentences** (ones that begin with *there* or *here*), find the subject by crossing out the expletive (*there* or *here*) and rearranging the sentence:

 1) ***There*** are more chairs in the other room.
 More chairs are in the other room.

 2) ***There*** is a whole pie left over.
 A whole pie is left over.

Expletive sentences are also called **inverted sentences**.

Imperative (Command) Sentences

Imperative sentences give instructions or commands. Consequently, the sentence begins with a verb. In this type of sentence, the subject is understood to be *you*.

 1) Finish your vegetables.
 (***You***) finish your vegetables.

 2) Respect your elders.
 (***You***) respect your elders.

It's Your Turn
Simple Subjects and Complete Subjects

■ Practice

Directions: Circle the simple subjects in the following sentences. Underline the complete subjects.

<u>The strongest (**man**) in the world</u> is the man who stands alone. —*Henrik Ibsen*

1. Time is the most valuable thing a man can spend. —*Theophrastus*

2. Beware the fury of a patient man. —*John Dryden*

3. Every society honors its live conformists and its dead troublemakers.
   —*Mignon McLaughlin*

4. There was never a great genius without a tincture of madness. —*Aristotle*

5. Why did the chicken cross the road?

■ Write Your Own

Directions: On a separate sheet of paper, finish the following sentences by inserting a complete subject.

1. _____ arrives at midnight.

2. _____ left without a trace.

3. _____ would have preferred a simple meal.

4. _____ had never thought to include President Clinton.

5. _____ absolutely, positively knew her time was at hand.

6. _____ was guilty of wishful thinking.

7. _____ hoped the spare ribs would win the prize.

8. _____ knew the secret to life.

9. _____ gave the wheel a spin.

10. _____ talked his way out, again.

Predicates

Predicates consist of the verb and its objects, complements, and modifiers. Predicates explain what the subject is *doing* or *being*.

Simple Predicates

The predicate may be a single word (**simple**), as in this sentence:

It ***rained***.

Complete Predicates

The predicate may also be long and complicated (**complete**), as in this sentence:

The soccer tournament ***<u>was held early in June at the Air Force Academy</u>***.

Whether the predicate is a single word or multiple words, it must complete the idea the subject begins. To find the predicate, ask *who* or *what* the subject is *doing* or *being*.

1) The waiter ***spilled*** water on Marsha's head.
   (What did the waiter do? Spilled water on Marsha's head.)

2) Happiness ***is*** a state of mind.
   (Happiness what? Is a state of mind.)

3) In the beginning, we ***couldn't*** decide which car to buy.
   (What couldn't we do? Decide which car to buy.)

Compound Predicates

Compound predicates (two or more simple predicates) are joined by the **coordinating conjunctions** *and, or, but,* or *nor*. No comma is used between the predicates unless three or more predicates are used.

1) Ted ***planned to mow the lawn*** but ***took a nap instead***. (two predicates)

2) On our last vacation, we ***camped in the Rockies***, ***rafted down the Colorado***, and ***hiked the Grand Canyon***. (three predicates)

The Grammar Notebook   ECS Learning Systems, Inc.

It's Your Turn
Complete Subjects and Complete Predicates

■ Practice

Directions: Underline the complete subjects and circle the complete predicates in the following sentences.

1. Boundaries create freedom. —*Anonymous*

2. Life and business are like the car pool lane. The best way to reach your destination quickly is to take some people with you. —*Pete Ward*

3 Take risks. You can't fall off the bottom. —*Barbara Proctor*

4. People who never get carried away should be. —*Malcolm Forbes*

5 *USA Today* has come out with a new survey. Apparently, three out of every four people make up 75% of the population. —*David Letterman*

6. The mind is an iceberg. It floats with only one-seventh of its bulk above water.
   —*Sigmund Freud*

7. The torments of martyrdom are probably most keenly felt by the bystanders.
   —*Ralph Waldo Emerson*

8. Leadership in today's world requires far more than a large stock of gunboats and a hard fist at the conference table. —*Hubert H. Humphrey*

9. Skepticism is the beginning of faith. —*Oscar Wilde*

10. An hour on the lake is like a day in the city. —*Greg Henry Quinn*

■ Write Your Own

Directions: Turn the following phrases into complete sentences by adding complete predicates. Write your answers on a separate sheet of paper.

1. The Everglades

2. My cousin

3. The Picasso painting

4. After work, we

5. The icing on the angel food cake

The Grammar Notebook   ECS Learning Systems, Inc.

Subject/Verb Agreement

Singular subjects use **singular verbs**. **Plural subjects** use **plural verbs**. For most native speakers of English, this is obvious and easy. Occasionally, though, the choice isn't so obvious. The most typical problems occur because of one of the following:

- the sentence includes *either/or* or *neither/nor*

- the subject is separated from the verb

- the verb comes before the subject

- collective nouns are used

- words with plural forms are used as singular units

Either...or, neither...nor

When *or* or *nor* connect compound subjects, the verb should agree with the subject closest to the verb. When both subjects are singular or both are plural, this is logical. If one subject is singular and the other is plural, this may sound wrong, even if it is grammatically correct:

> Neither *Allen* nor *his employees* <u>are</u> planning to work on Saturday.
>   singular   plural   plural
>   subject   subject   verb

> Neither *his employees* nor *Allen* <u>is</u> planning to work on Saturday.
>   plural   singular singular
>   subject   subject   verb

Even though both are correct, the first sentence generally sounds better to our ears. This is because we pick up on the compound subjects and don't pay any attention to whether they are joined by *and*, *or*, or *nor*.

■ Tip

> To test for the correct verb, put your finger over the sentence up to the final subject, then read. Does the verb agree with the subject? If *yes*, then you are grammatically correct. If the sentence is jarring to your ears, reverse the subjects.

ECS Learning Systems, Inc. The Grammar Notebook

~~Neither the students nor~~ the teacher is ready for vacation to end. (Correct but jarring to the ear.)

~~Neither the teacher nor~~ the students are ready for vacation to end. (Correct and not jarring.)

Subject Separated from the Verb

Subjects are often separated from the verb by **prepositional phrases** or **relative clauses**. No matter how many words come between the two, the verb must still agree with the subject. The difficulty comes when the words in the phrase or clause differ in number from the subject:

A <u>subject</u> *that is separated from the verb by phrases or clauses* <u>is</u> common.
| singular | relative Clause | singular |
| subject | | verb |

Pronouns separated from their verbs can be particularly troublesome if they are **indefinite pronouns** (*anyone, somebody, someone,* etc.). Most indefinite pronouns are singular, although we often use them as singular or plural in informal speech.

<u>Anybody</u> *who wants to go to the zoo with the children* <u>is</u> welcome to come.
| singular | relative Clause | singular |
| subject | | verb |

■ Tip

To find the correct verb form, cross out the phrase or clause that comes between the two and read.

Anybody ~~who wants to go to the zoo with the children~~ is welcome to come.

Verb Before the Subject

In some sentences, the verb comes before the subject. The most common examples are in **questions** and **expletive (or inverted) sentences,** which use *there/here is* and *there/here are* (or *there/here was* and *there/here were*). To determine subjects and verbs, turn questions into statements and rearrange expletive sentences, deleting *there is* and *there are*.

ECS Learning Systems, Inc.

Questions

What *is* the main *reason* writers become confused?
     singular   singular
     verb   subject

Rearranged: The main *reason* writers become confused *is* this.
             subject   verb

Inverted Sentences (Expletive Construction):

There are a *child* and *his parents* here to see the doctor.
   verb subject   subject

Rearranged: *A child* and *his parents are* here to see the doctor.
         subject   subject   verb

Collective Nouns

Collective nouns can act as either a single unit and take a **singular verb** or act as individuals within a unit and take a **plural verb**. Common collective nouns are *committee, jury, crowd, audience, family,* and *couple.*

Although sports teams could be considered singular collective nouns, they always take a plural verb.

> *The couple resides* at 100 W. Pikes Peak Avenue.
>   [*it*] resides

> *The couple are* disagreeing about where to live.
>   [*they*] are disagreeing

Even though the second sentence is grammatically correct, it sounds wrong. To stay grammatically correct and avoid a strange-sounding sentence, rearrange it. The following are several options:

1) The husband and wife *are disagreeing* about where to live.

2) The two *are disagreeing* about where to live.

3) They *are disagreeing* about where to live.

Some words with plural forms are used as singular units. Words such as *measles, mumps, economics, statistics, mathematics, athletics,* and so on, take singular verb forms even though they end in **s.**

1) *Mumps* can be a deadly disease in adults.

2) *Economics* is fascinating when taught by a good teacher.

It's Your Turn
Subject/Verb Agreement

■ Practice

Directions: Circle the correct form of the verb. Explain which rule applies.

Athletics (*come*)/*comes* easily for Meryl.
(**Rule**: The word *athletics* is a singular unit.)

1. The committee *is/are* planning to celebrate its success.

2. Who *is/are* the winners of the Nobel Prize this year?

3. There *is/are* no such thing as a minor lapse of integrity. —*Tom Peters*

4. Approximately 40 percent of all American households *has/have* a computer.

5. Either the office staff or Pat *closes/close* up every night.

6. The perception of the Soviets that has developed over the past 50 years *is/are* difficult to change.

7. Neither mumps nor measles *is/are* usually lethal.

8. The jury *is/are* arguing heatedly over the defendant's guilt or innocence.

9. Mathematics *is/are* challenging.

10. The people I know who are the most generous *is/are* the ones who have the least.

■ Write Your Own

Directions: On a separate sheet of paper, write sentences using a present tense verb for the following prompts.

1. Use *economics* as the subject.
2. Use a collective noun in which the individuals in the unit do not act as a single unit.
3. Use an inverted sentence structure.
4. Separate the subject from the verb with the phrase *who would challenge the rights of parents*.
5. Use *the Broncos* as the subject.
6. Use *either … or* to separate compound subjects.
7. Use an inverted sentence structure with *skiers* and *slope* in the sentence.
8. Use *audience* as the subject of a sentence.

Review

■ What Have You Learned So Far?

Directions: Reflect on what you have learned so far. Think about these questions as you answer the questions below: What has been easy to learn? What has been difficult? What most helps you to learn? What can you do to improve how you're learning?

1. What have you learned about subjects and predicates?

2. How has this changed your use of language?

3. What are you still not sure about? How will you gain clarification?

4. What additional information do you want to learn about subjects and predicates?

ECS Learning Systems, Inc.

Language Play:
English as the Official Language

From time to time, there is a public outcry for passing a law that makes English the official language of the United States. The assumption behind this is that if we don't make the U.S. a one-language country, pretty soon English speakers will be the minority. In the U.S., we don't require that students become proficient in two languages. Perhaps we should make more of an effort to encourage non-English speakers to retain their home language as well as learn English.

Explore

A. What would be the benefits of an "English-only" law? What would be the disadvantages? Does the United States need such a law?

B. Do we have more difficulty with immigrants not learning English than previous generations? What opportunities do immigrants now have to learn English that previous generations didn't have?

C. What disadvantages do immigrants have that previous generations didn't have? What impact does the language of immigrants have on the internal history of English?

D. How might someone living in Miami, urban California, or along the Texas-Mexico border view an English-only law differently than someone living in rural Nebraska?

ECS Learning Systems, Inc.   The Grammar Notebook

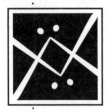

Clauses

Clauses are groups of words containing a complete subject and a predicate. There are two kinds of clauses: **independent** and **dependent**.

Independent Clauses

An independent clause can stand by itself as a sentence. It is a complete idea.

> The Colorado Springs city council decided to spell Pikes Peak without an apostrophe.

Independent clauses may have compound subjects or predicates or both.

> *Journalists* and *teachers* <u>*wrote*</u> letters and <u>*protested*</u>.
>   subject   subject predicate   predicate

Dependent Clauses

Although a **dependent clause** has a subject and a predicate, it cannot stand by itself. It depends on an independent clause to complete the thought.

A dependent clause may also be called a **subordinate clause** because it subordinates one idea to another. The following are examples of subordinate clauses. (Remember, length has nothing to do with whether the clause is independent or dependent. If the clause is a complete idea, it is independent. If it cannot stand on its own, it is dependent.)

Examples:
1) when the police arrived
2) after we exchanged insurance cards
3) while we waited for the tow truck
4) whose sister knew the phone number
5) why she waited so long
6) because she ate the last piece of pie
7) although it seemed a good idea at the time
8) whenever they get the urge
9) until he stops
10) how they made ends meet

The Grammar Notebook   ECS Learning Systems, Inc.

■ Tip

> The relative pronoun *that* is sometimes deleted when the sentence is clear without it:
>
> > To make certain [**that**] crime doesn't pay, the government should take it over and run it.—*US News*

Noun, Adjective, and Adverb Clauses

Noun clauses function as nouns in a sentence. They generally begin with a **relative pronoun** or a **subordinating conjunction** such as *how*, *when*, *where*, *whether*, or *why*. Although none of the three kinds of clauses can stand by themselves, noun clauses play different roles in sentences than adverb or adjective clauses.

Adverb and **adjective clauses** modify other words, phrases, or clauses. A noun clause, on the other hand, is used only in the way a noun is used, as a subject, subject complement, or object. Because noun clauses begin with the same kinds of words as adjective or adverb clauses, it may be confusing at first to determine which is which. Fortunately, there's a simple test. Just as a noun can always be replaced by a pronoun, so can a noun clause:

1) *What you see* is *what you get.*
   [*This*] is [*it*].

2) The professor explained *why the Serbs don't like the Bosnians.*
   The professor explained [*this*].

■ Tip

> A noun clause, even though it is a dependent clause, must always be *within* an independent clause. Often, the independent clause would not make sense without it. In contrast, if adverb and adjective clauses are taken out of a sentence, the sentence will still be grammatically correct, even if it's not informationally complete.

Noun clause: What the doctor said is important.
What the doctor said ~~is important~~.

Adjective clause: The man who left early is a new employee.
The man ~~who left early~~ is a new employee.

Adverb clause: The car ran out of gas before I reached the gas station.
The car ran out of gas ~~before I reached the gas station~~.

It's Your Turn
Clauses

■ Practice

Directions: Circle the dependent clauses. Identify whether the dependent clause is an adverb, adjective, or noun clause.

The people (who change best and fastest) are the ones (who have no choice.)
          adjective   adjective

1. What gets measured becomes important.

2. The value of an employee is not in what he can do but what he is willing to do.
    —*Virginia Rich*

3. It's easier for people to see it your way if you first see it their way. —*Jack Kaine*

4. Some succeed because they are destined to; most succeed because they are determined to. —*Anatole France*

5. A college education seldom hurts a man if he's willing to learn a little something after he graduates.

6. I had a monumental idea this morning, but I didn't like it. —*Samuel Goldwyn*

7. The secret of managing is to keep the guys who hate you away from the guys who are undecided. —*Casey Stengel*

8. If you're too busy to help those around you succeed, you're too busy. —*Bob Moawad*

9. How we get to where we don't know we're going determines where we end up.

10. It's not what you tell them that counts. It's what they take away.

■ Write Your Own

Directions: On a separate sheet of paper, write three sentences using independent clauses, three sentences using dependent clauses (adverb or adjective), and three sentences using noun clauses. Underline the independent clauses.

The Grammar Notebook   ECS Learning Systems, Inc.

Sentence Fragments

A **sentence fragment** is a group of words that is typically a dependent clause or a phrase. The group of words either lack a subject and verb or begin with a subordinating conjunction and is a dependent clause. Even though a fragment is one of the most glaring errors a writer can make, fortunately it is also one of the easiest to fix. The following are the three most common ways to turn a fragment into a complete sentence.

1) Attach a dependent clause to an independent clause that comes before or after the dependent clause.

   No: *Although the boys played rough.* The girls played rougher.
   Yes: Although the boys played rough, the girls played rougher.

   No: Dinner will get cold. *If Steve doesn't get here soon.*
   Yes: Dinner will get cold if Steve doesn't get here soon.

2) Attach a phrase to an independent clause, or turn it into a complete thought by adding a subject and verb.

   No: Chasms need to be leaped in one big jump. *Not two smaller ones.*
   Yes: Chasms need to be leaped in one big jump, not two smaller ones.

   No: The best listeners have one thing in common. *Having an open mind.*
   Yes: The best listeners have one thing in common: having an open mind.

   No: *One that is more difficult than all the others combined.*
   Yes: It's one that is more difficult than all the others combined.

3) Attach word groups to an independent clause, or turn it into a complete thought by adding a subject and verb.

   No: Some of his biggest fears never materialized. *Such as, losing his job, going bankrupt, and crashing his truck.*
   Yes: Some of his biggest fears never materialized, such as losing his job, going bankrupt, and crashing his truck.

   No: In addition, *revealing his soft heart.*
   Yes: In addition, he worried about revealing his soft heart.

■ Tip

Sometimes writers use fragments intentionally as a way to grab the reader's attention. As with any attention-grabbing technique, use this one sparingly and deliberately!

　　　ECS Learning Systems, Inc.　　　The Grammar Notebook

It's Your Turn
Sentence Fragments

■ Practice

Directions: On a separate sheet of paper, rewrite the following into complete sentences. There may be more than one right answer.

> **Incomplete:** So that everyone would have an equal chance.
>
> **Complete:** So that everyone would have an equal chance, the children took turns.
> —or—
> The children took turns so that everyone would have an equal chance.

1. Timing the races at the track meet last spring.

2. Although more people prefer Wonder bread.

3. Screaming at the top of their lungs as they flew wildly along on the roller coaster.

4. Reworking my term paper in the hopes the teacher would approve of the new draft.

5. Pleasant dreams to all little children.

6. While most people would have chosen the other road.

7. Candidates who run in a national election.

8. Because Dad accidentally left his wallet at home.

9. Sharing desk space and battling for locker space every day with my best friend.

10. Hanging by a thread.

Phrases

Phrases, in contrast to clauses, do not have subjects or predicates. Sometimes phrases are confused with clauses. This is usually because, as with independent and dependent clauses, length is not the determining factor. Clauses can either be long or contain three or four words. Phrases, although usually short, can also be lengthy. Phrases may also include gerunds, participles, or infinitives, which are sometimes confused with verbs. The following are common kinds of phrases.

Prepositional Phrases

Prepositional phrases begin with a preposition and end with a noun or pronoun. They function either as adjectives or adverbs. When functioning as adjectives, they almost always follow the nouns or pronouns they modify. When functioning as adverbs, they can be moved around in the sentence.

> **Adjective:** The store *on the corner* sells used books. (Which store?)
> **Adverb:** Russia's future will be decided *by a run-off election*. (How will it be decided?)

Gerund Phrases

A **gerund** is the present participle form of a word formed by adding *-ing* to its base form. A **gerund phrase** is a gerund along with its complements and modifiers. **Gerund phrases** always function as nouns. As a noun, a gerund phrase may be a subject, subject complement, or an object. As with any other noun, the easiest test for a gerund phrase is to replace the phrase with a pronoun. If the sentence still makes sense, the word is a gerund.

> *Eating watermelon* can be messy.
> [This] can be messy.

ECS Learning Systems, Inc.

Participle Phrases

A **participle** is the present or past participle form of a word (verbs most commonly ending in *-ing* and *-ed*). A **participle phrase** is a participle along with its complements and modifiers. **Participle phrases** always function as adjectives. They usually follow the nouns or pronouns they modify, but unlike other words, phrases, or clauses that function as adjectives, they can move around. They can precede or even be separated from the words they modify.

1) The children, *dreaming of sugarplums*, slept restlessly. (modifies *children*)

2) *Coming in torrents*, the rain quickly flooded the streets. (modifies *rain*)

3) Life is a game of cards, *dealt by someone else*. (modifies *cards*)

Infinitive Phrases

An **infinitive phrase** includes the infinitive form of the verb along with its complements and modifiers. **Infinitive phrases** can function as nouns, adjectives, or adverbs. When they function as adjectives, they usually follow the nouns or pronouns they modify.

Noun: My mother decided *to plant gladiola bulbs this spring*.

Adjective: He gave me the chance *to learn from my mistakes*. (modifies *chance*)

Adverb: He left *to begin life on his own*. (explains why he left)

■ Tip

Both **prepositional phrases** and **infinitive phrases** can begin with the word *to*. When a noun follows *to*, it is a prepositional phrase. When a verb follows *to*, it is an infinitive phrase.

Prepositional phrase: Angie drove *to Denver*.

Infinitive phrase: Sean wanted *to drive*.

ECS Learning Systems, Inc.

It's Your Turn
Phrases

■ Practice

Directions: Underline the phrases in the following sentences. Identify whether they are prepositional, gerund, participle, or infinitive phrases.

> <u>Winning the pennant</u> cost the team everything.
> **gerund**

1. Beware of Greeks bearing gifts.

2. Mother always said to treat others in the way we wanted to be treated.

3. Lisa's favorite pastime is surfing the Internet.

4. Sleeping under the table, the kittens seemed content.

5. She spends most of the morning at her office.

6. For example, Tom is planning to paint the house.

7. Considering the odds, we were surprised to win the lottery twice in a year.

8. Simple, clear purpose and principles give rise to complex and intelligent behavior. Complex rules and regulations give rise to simple and stupid behavior. —*Dee Hock*

9. Explorers have to be ready to die lost. —*Russell Hoban*

10. In the end, it is attention to detail that makes all the difference. —*David Noonan*

■ Write Your Own

Directions: On a separate sheet of paper, write sentences that include the following types of phrases. Underline and identify the phrases in each sentence.

1. Prepositional phrase

2. Gerund phrase

3. Participle phrase

4. Infinitive phrase

ECS Learning Systems, Inc. The Grammar Notebook

Sentence Structures

A, B, C, D, and E

Traditional grammar books classify sentences into four structures: **simple**, **compound**, **complex**, and **compound-complex**. These structures are based on various combinations of independent and dependent clauses. This is a helpful system because it gives writers an understanding of how to manipulate clauses and create more interesting sentences.

The system falls short, however, of explaining how to punctuate the sentences. The system on the following pages explains both: how to combine clauses into more effective sentences *and* how to punctuate them correctly.

The Grammar Notebook ECS Learning Systems, Inc.

If you are familiar with the traditional sentence classification, the following table will help you connect what you know to what you're about to learn.

Traditional/*Grammar Notebook* Sentence Structure Classification

Traditional Sentence Classification (Simple, Compound, Complex, Compound-Complex)	*Grammar Notebook* Sentence Classification (A, B, C, D, E)
Simple • one independent clause with no dependent clauses • no internal punctuation	**A:** The dog barked. The cat fainted.
Compound • two or more independent clauses with no dependent clauses • connected by a comma and a coordinating conjunction (*for, and, nor, but, or, yet, so*)	**B:** The dog barked, and the cat fainted.
Complex • one independent clause and one or more dependent clauses • may or may not need internal punctuation (parentheses or pair of commas or dashes) • dependent clause signaled by subordinating conjunction • may contain independent clause with a restrictive (necessary) interruption between subject and predicate	**C:** The cat fainted because the dog barked. **D:** When the dog barked, the cat fainted. **E:** The cat, who needed therapy, fainted.
Compound Complex • Two or more independent clauses and one or more dependent clauses followed by a dependent adverbial clause • Dependent clause signaled by subordinating conjunction • May contain internal punctuation (parentheses or a pair of commas or dashes)	Combinations of **B** with **C, D,** and **E.** **Examples:** • When the dog barked, the cat fainted and panic ensued. • The movie which stars Jimmy Stewart has become a classic. • The campsite was beautiful—despite its distance from the road—and we had a great time.

ECS Learning Systems, Inc.   The Grammar Notebook

Sentence Structure A

Features

a. one independent clause that expresses a single and complete idea

b. complete subject and complete predicate

c. no internal punctuation unless there is a list

d. a simple sentence

Examples: 1) It is hard to be good. —*Pittacus*

Complete subject = *It*
Complete predicate = *is hard to be good*

2) The chief function of your body is to carry your brain around. —*Edison*

Complete subject = *The chief function of your body*
Complete predicate = *is to carry your brain around*

3) Genius is an African who dreams up snow. —*Vladimir Nabokov*

Complete subject = *Genius*
Complete predicate = *is an African who dreams up snow*

What to Watch Out For

Unnecessary Commas

One temptation many writers have is to insert a comma wherever they think readers may need to breathe. It isn't necessary to remind them to do this since most people are able to read and breathe at the same time. In fact, if the writer uses too many commas, readers may become confused.

A Structure sentences often fall victim to extra commas because writers worry about long strings of words with no breaks. The most frequent temptation is to put commas between compound elements, treating them like a list. The following sentence illustrates this.

America is a country that doesn't know where it is going but is determined to set a speed record getting there. —*Lawrence J. Peter*

You may be tempted to insert a comma between *going* and *but*. However, the sentence does not need a comma because it doesn't list items in a series. It has only two elements:

1) *doesn't know where it is going*

2) *is determined to set a speed record getting there*

The sentence also has only one independent clause. If the sentence were to read as follows, then a comma would become necessary between the two independent clauses:

America is a country that doesn't know where it is going, but *it* is determined to set a speed record getting there.

Likewise, if a third element is added to the list, a comma may be used.

America is a country that doesn't know where it is going, is determined to set a speed record getting there, and will be surprised about wherever it arrives.

■ Discuss

Some writers consider that the word *and* eliminates the need for a comma before the last item in a series. However, for no more work than it takes to insert a comma, adding one before the final item in a list also adds clarity to the sentence.

Examples:

Patrice invited the *Sanchezes*, Tom and Susan. (Patrice invited Tom and Susan *Sanchez*.)

Patrice invited the *Sanchezes*, *Tom*, and *Susan*. (Patrice invited the *Sanchezes*. She also invited Tom and Susan.)

ECS Learning Systems, Inc.   The Grammar Notebook

It's Your Turn
Sentence Structure A

■ Practice

Directions: Put an "A" beside the A Structure sentences.

1. _____ A fool and his money are soon partying.

2. _____ If you think education is expensive, try ignorance.

3. _____ Visualize whirled peas.

4. _____ Don't believe everything you think.

5. _____ When all is said and done, more is said than done.

6. _____ The only way to have a friend is to be one. —*Emerson*

7. _____ Eighty percent of success is showing up. —*Woody Allen*

8. _____ Nobody who has not been in the interior of a family can say what the difficulties of any individual of that family may be. —*Jane Austen*

9. _____ When you come to a fork in the road, take it. —*Yogi Berra*

10. _____ A fanatic is one who can't change his mind and won't change the subject.
    —*Winston Churchill*

■ Write Your Own

Directions: On a separate sheet of paper, write five A Structure sentences of your own. For two of the sentences, choose very simple, related sentences.

Examples: 1) The dog barked.

2) The cat fainted.

Sentence Structure B

Features

a. two or more independent clauses that can stand individually

b. and a coordinating conjunction (*for, and, nor, but, or, yet, so*: FANBOYS)

c. clauses may be joined by a semicolon (;), colon (:), or dash (—) instead of the comma and the coordinating conjunction

d. clauses that may be joined by a semicolon (;), conjunctive adverb (*however, therefore, moreover*, etc.) or transitional phrase, and a comma

e. two equal and related clauses

f. a compound sentence

Examples:

1) Everyone is a genius at least once a year; a real genius has his original ideas closer together. —*G.C. Lichtenberg*

   Independent clause = *Everyone is a genius at least once a year*
   Independent clause = *a real genius has his original ideas closer together*

2) Knowledge may give weight, but accomplishments give luster, and many more people see than weigh.
                                —*Philip Dormer Stanhope, Earl of Chesterfield*

   Independent clause = *Knowledge may give weight*
   Independent clause = *accomplishments give luster*
   Independent clause = *many more people see than weigh*

3) Don't go around saying the world owes you a living; the world owes you nothing; it was here first. —*Mark Twain*

   Independent clause = *Don't go around saying the world owes you a living*

   Independent clause = *the world owes you nothing*

   Independent clause = *it was here first*

ECS Learning Systems, Inc.   The Grammar Notebook

What to Watch Out For

Run-on Sentences

In B Structure sentences, some mistakes are greater than others. The most troublesome error for the reader happens when two independent clauses are placed back to back with no punctuation between them:

> **No:** A soft answer turneth away wrath grievous words stir up anger. —*Proverbs 15:1*

> **Yes:** A soft answer turneth away wrath, but grievous words stir up anger.

The first sentence is called a **run-on sentence**. More than any mistake (other than a fragment), it forces the reader to work too hard to understand what the writer means to say. Fortunately, this problem is easily fixed. Inserting any one of the following will quickly remedy the error:

1) **Semicolon**: A soft answer turneth away wrath; grievous words stir up anger.

2) **Semicolon, conjunctive adverb**: A soft answer turneth away wrath; however, grievous words stir up anger.

3) **Colon**: A soft answer turneth away wrath: grievous words stir up anger.

4) **Dash**: A soft answer turneth away wrath—grievous words stir up anger.

5) **Period and capital**: A soft answer turneth away wrath. Grievous words stir up anger.

6) **Comma and a coordinating conjunction**: A soft answer turneth away wrath, but grievous words stir up anger.

■ Discuss

> Each method of dividing the two clauses creates a slightly different impact. What differences do you see? (For instance, which are formal or wordy or easiest to read?)
>
> Generally, using a semicolon and conjunctive adverb produces a more formal, academic-sounding sentence, while the dash seems more informal. Separating the clauses into two sentences can make them choppy. Conversely, adding the comma and a coordinating conjunction can make the sentence unnecessarily wordy. Although all of these are grammatically correct ways of writing the B Structure sentence, some choices produce punchier sentences than others.

ECS Learning Systems, Inc.

Comma Splices

Writers often make the mistake of putting two independent clauses together into a single sentence and joining them with only a comma, rather than a comma and a coordinating conjunction. In grammatical terms this is called a **comma splice**. Because a comma is not strong enough punctuation to hold two clauses together, a comma splice is considered a major error or a minor grammatical *faux pas* (depending on the social circles in which the writer travels). The exception to this is when the independent clauses are short and parallel in construction, as in the following:

> We came, we saw, we ate.

Here, either semicolons or the coordinating conjunction would pointlessly slow down the reader, and the sentence would lose its crispness. Likewise, separating the clauses into individual sentences would make them too choppy.

Using Semicolons

In the most typical mistake, writers join independent clauses with a coordinating conjunction but leave out the comma. Again, exceptions to this rule exist. As with a comma splice, when short, parallel independent clauses are joined, the comma may be dropped. This is not only forgivable but also sometimes preferable if the extra punctuation would slow the reader down. While a comma between the first and second clauses would not be wrong, it just isn't necessary. The following sentence illustrates this nicely:

> I've been rich and I've been poor; rich is better. —*Sophie Tucker*

Notice how the sentence would read with a comma and a coordinating conjunction (most logically the word *but*) instead of the semicolon:

> I've been rich and I've been poor, but rich is better.

The second sentence reads like a popped balloon. The semicolon in the original pulls the third clause in tight and clean, forcing the reader to sit up and pay attention to the final clause.

When semicolons are used correctly, they add polish and sophistication to writing. When used incorrectly, the misuse can be glaring. To determine when to use a semicolon, writers should always abide by this rule of thumb:

> Except for between items in a series, an independent clause should always come before and after a semicolon.

■ Tip

> The best test for using a semicolon is to replace it with a period. If no fragment appears, the semicolon may be used. If one of the clauses turns into a fragment, a comma is probably the correct punctuation.

Using Colons

In a B Structure sentence, an independent clause must come before and after the colon. However, in other sentences, the colon has a little more flexibility. Unfortunately, this results in abuse as well. Any grammar book will say that an independent clause always comes before a colon. A single word, list, phrase, or independent clause may come after a colon. This means that a colon should never follow the verb.

> **Incorrect:** Students need: pencils, paper, books, and thinking caps.

> **Correct:** Students need pencils, paper, books, and thinking caps.

As with the semicolon, the best test for whether or not a colon is correct is to put a period in place of the colon. If the clause before the colon is independent, a colon is correct. If the reader is left hanging, it's incorrect. Having said all of this, it's worth noting that standards for using the colon are changing. It is not uncommon—although still not technically correct—to see the colon used instead of a comma after an introductory word phrase such as the following:

> Without a doubt: punctuation rules are changing.

The first word after the colon may or may not be capitalized. However, the writer should be consistent.

ECS Learning Systems, Inc.

It's Your Turn
Sentence Structures A and B

■ Practice

Directions: Identify which of the following sentences are A Structure (A) and which are B Structure sentences (B). Punctuate each sentence appropriately.

_____ 1. Familiarity breeds contempt.

_____ 2. Everything that irritates us about others can lead us to an understanding of ourselves. —*Morton Hunt*

_____ 3. Choose your life's mate carefully from this one decision will come ninety percent of all your happiness or misery. —*Jackson Browne, Jr.*

_____ 4. To love and to be loved is to feel the sun from both sides. —*David Viscott*

_____ 5. It is not easy to find happiness in ourselves and it is not possible to find it elsewhere. —*Agnes Repplier*

_____ 6. The basic purpose of a liberal arts education is to liberate the human being to exercise his or her potential to the fullest. —*Barbara M. White*

_____ 7. No man sees far most see no farther than their noses. —*Thomas Carlyle*

_____ 8. Chance is a word void of sense nothing can exist without a cause. —*Voltaire*

_____ 9. What we anticipate seldom occurs what we least expect generally happens.
                        —*Benjamin Disraeli*

_____ 10. Regret is an appalling waste of energy you can't build on it it is good only for wallowing in. —*Katherine Mansfield*

ECS Learning Systems, Inc.   The Grammar Notebook

■ Write Your Own

Directions: On a separate sheet of paper, write five B Structure sentences of your own.

Examples: 1) The dog barked, and the cat fainted.

2) The dog barked; the cat fainted.

3) The dog barked; therefore, the cat fainted.

The Grammar Notebook   ECS Learning Systems, Inc.

Sentence Structure C

Features

a. independent clause followed by a dependent adverbial clause

b. dependent clause signaled by a subordinating conjunction

c. no internal punctuation between clauses (exceptions: clauses beginning with *although*, *even though*, *as if*, and *even if* may sometimes require a comma)

d. complex sentence structure

Examples: 1) No man can think clearly when his fists are clenched.
—*George Jean Nathan*

   Independent clause = *No man can think clearly*
   Dependent clause = *when his fists are clenched*

2) A fanatic is someone who redoubles his efforts when he's forgotten his aim. —*Chuck Jones*

   Independent clause = *A fanatic is someone*
   Dependent clause = *who redoubles his efforts*
   Dependent clause = *when he's forgotten his aim*

3) Three may keep a secret if two of them are dead. —*Benjamin Franklin*

   Independent clause = *Three may keep a secret*
   Dependent clause = *if two of them are dead*

What To Watch Out For

Punctuation Between Clauses

C Structure sentences can sometimes be tricky. Writers with unpracticed ears are often tempted to put commas between independent and dependent clauses. Keep in mind that commas always have a purpose. They help the reader avoid confusion by signaling that the focus of the sentence is shifting. Although adding a comma unnecessarily between an independent and dependent clause in a C Structure sentence is not as confusing as it is in some of the other sentence structures, the rule of thumb is to use less punctuation rather than more. Commas slow the reader down. If readers don't need to pause, the writer should make every effort not to slow the reader down with unnecessary punctuation.

Using *That, So,* and *So that*

Watch, too, for sentences where the subordinating conjunction is understood. The most common example of this is the subordinating conjunction *that*. If a dependent clause reads clearly and means the same thing with or without *that*, remove it. Always opt for the shorter version, as in the following:

1) A man will pay $2 for a $1 item he wants. A woman will pay $1 for a $2 item she doesn't want. —*Wal-Mart's chairman, on the nature of Christmas shopping, US News*

   Independent clause = *A man will pay $2 for a $1 item*
   Dependent clause = *[that] he wants*
   Independent clause = *A woman will pay $1 for a $2 item*
   Dependent clause = *[that] she doesn't want*

2) Many a man has fallen in love with a girl in a light so dim he would not have chosen a suit by it. —*Maurice Chevalier*

   Independent clause = *Many a man has fallen in love with a girl in a light so dim*
   Dependent clause = *[that] he would not have chosen a suit by it*

In both examples, the reader understands the meaning without having to read the sentence twice. Thus, the sentences are stronger and clearer without *that*.

In addition, writers may be confused about when to use *so* and *so that*. The distinction is important because *so* separates independent clauses and requires a comma, while *so that* separates an independent clause from a dependent clause and does not take a comma. To remember when to use each one, think of *so* as *therefore* and think of *so that* as *in order to* or *in order that*. The following sentences illustrate the difference.

1) We left home early, **so** we were one of the first in line at the theater.
   (We left home early; **therefore**, we were one of the first in line at the theater.)

2) We left home early **so that** we could be one of the first in line at the theater.
   (We left home early **in order** to be one of the first in line at the theater.)

■ Tip

The most common subordinating conjunctions are as follows:

after	before	so that	where
although	even though	though	whereas
as	if	unless	wherever
as if	in order that	until	whether
as though	rather than	when	while
because	since	whenever	why

ECS Learning Systems, Inc.

It's Your Turn
Sentence Structures A, B, and C

■ Practice

Directions: Identify the following as A, B, or C Structure sentences. Underline the independent clauses once and the dependent clauses twice. Punctuate each sentence correctly.

_____ 1. Can anybody remember when times were not hard and money not scarce? —*Ralph Waldo Emerson*

_____ 2. Problems can become opportunities when the right people come together. —*Robert Redford*

_____ 3. Very little is needed to make a happy life. —*Marcus Aurelius Antonius*

_____ 4. Seize the day put no trust in the morrow. —*Horace*

_____ 5. Our duty is to proceed as if limits to our ability do not exist. —*Teilhard de Chardin*

_____ 6. You can outdo you if you really want to. —*Paul Harvey*

_____ 7. There is no traffic jam on the extra mile.

_____ 8. One person can make a difference and every person should try. —*John F. Kennedy*

_____ 9. We must learn to lift as we climb. —*Angela Davis*

_____ 10. There are no exceptions to the rule that everybody likes to be an exception to the rule. —*Malcolm Forbes*

■ Write Your Own

Directions: On a separate sheet of paper, write five C Structure sentences of your own. Create new ones by patterning the sentences off of the practice sentences above.

Examples: 1) The dog barked when the cat fainted.

                   2) The cat fainted because the dog barked.

Sentence Structure D

Features

a. single word, phrase, or dependent adverbial clause followed by an independent clause

b. dependent clause generally signaled by a subordinating conjunction

c. two parts separated by a comma

Examples: 1) If all economists were laid end to end, they would not reach a conclusion. —*George Bernard Shaw*

Dependent clause = *If all economists were laid to end*
Independent clause = *they would not reach a conclusion*

2) When choosing between two evils, I always like to try the one I've never tried before. —*Mae West*

Phrase = *When choosing between two evils*
Independent clause = *I always like to try the one*
Dependent clause = *[that] I've never tried before*

3) In general, the art of government consists in taking as much money as possible from one class of citizens to give it to the other. —*Voltaire*

Phrase = *In general*
Independent clause = *the art of government consists in taking as much money as possible from one class of citizens to give it to the other*

What to Watch Out For

Comma Omissions

Since the goal of a good writer is to make the reader's job as easy as possible, forgetting to put a comma in a D Structure sentence is a major error. Without the comma, the reader may have to read the sentence twice or may miss the meaning entirely. If you doubt the importance of the comma, read the following sentence:

While we were eating tarantulas migrated through our campsite.

Not only are readers forced to re-read the sentence and mentally insert a comma to understand it, they're also burdened with uneasy thoughts, for at least a moment, about the writer's culinary habits. At best, the writer creates more work for readers; at worst, the writer distracts them for the next several sentences and may never regain their interest.

Sometimes, the comma is not only important for easier reading, but it also impacts the meaning, as in the following two sentences:

Mary, read this.

Mary read this.

In the first sentence, Mary is being spoken to. In the second, she is being spoken about. Notice that the comma actually changes the pronunciation of *read*. Although this impact is rare, it nicely illustrates just how important the comma can be.

It's Your Turn
Sentence Structures A, B, C, and D

■ Practice

Directions: Identify the following as A, B, C, or D Structure sentences. Underline the independent clauses once and the dependent clauses twice. Circle introductory phrases or single words. Punctuate each sentence correctly.

_____ 1. If fifty million people say a foolish thing it is still a foolish thing. —*Anatole France*

_____ 2. Too many people think they are being creative when they are just being different.

_____ 3. To me old age is always fifteen years older than I am. —*Bernard Baruch*

_____ 4. Making the decision to have a child it's momentous. —*Elizabeth Stone*

_____ 5. Toto we're not in Kansas anymore. —*Dorothy in* The Wizard of Oz

_____ 6. The latter part of a wise man's life is taken up in curing the follies, prejudices, and false opinions he contracted in the former. —*Jonathan Swift*

_____ 7. Where all think alike no one thinks very much. —*Walter Lippmann*

_____ 8. If he works for you you work for him. —*Japanese Proverb*

_____ 9. Debate is masculine conversation is feminine. —*Amos Bronson Alcott*

_____ 10. Cauliflower is nothing but cabbage with a college education. —*Mark Twain*

■ Write Your Own

Directions: On a separate sheet of paper, write D Structure sentences of your own. Create new ones, patterning the sentences off of the practice sentences. Include sentences with an introductory word, a phrase, and an independent clause.

Examples: 1) After the cat fainted, the dog barked.

2) While barking, the dog watched the cat faint.

3) Today, the dog and cat had another episode.

ECS Learning Systems, Inc.

Sentence Structure E

Features

a. independent clause interrupted by unnecessary or nonrestrictive material

b. nonrestrictive (unnecessary) information always set off by a pair of commas, dashes, parentheses, or brackets if it comes between the subject and the predicate

Examples:

1) All government—indeed, every human benefit and enjoyment, every virtue and every prudent act—is founded on compromise and barter.
   —*Edmund Burke*

   Independent clause = *All government is founded on compromise and barter*
   Nonrestrictive (unnecessary) phrase = *indeed, every human benefit and enjoyment, every virtue and every prudent act*

2) Under enough pressure, most people—but not everybody—will stretch the truth on you. —US News

   Phrase = *Under enough pressure*
   Independent clause = *most people will stretch the truth on you*
   Nonrestrictive (unnecessary) phrase = *but not everybody*

Not E Structure sentence:

3) The movie which stars Jimmy Stewart has become a classic.

   Independent clause = *The movie has become a classic*
   Restrictive (necessary) dependent clause = *which stars*

What to Watch Out For

Punctuating Restrictive and Nonrestrictive Clauses

In E Structure sentence, anything between the commas can be deleted, and the sentence will still make sense grammatically and informationally. This is why the third sentence above is not an E Structure sentence, even though it contains a dependent clause between the subject and predicate. The information between the subject and predicate (*which stars*) helps to define the subject. This information is **restrictive** (necessary), and no commas should be used. When the

ECS Learning Systems, Inc. The Grammar Notebook

information between the subject and the predicate is **nonrestrictive** (not necessary), and a pair of commas should be used.

In addition, be careful not to separate the subject from the verb with a single comma. This would make no more sense to the careful reader than if the writer used only one parenthesis as in the following sentence:

> The future as Eleanor Roosevelt once said $\big)$ belongs to those who believe in the beauty of their dreams.

The single parenthesis is confusing. Good readers would stop and go back to look for the other parenthesis, knowing instinctively that they must have misread the information. A single comma between *said* and *belongs* would do the same thing to careful readers. If the writer thinks a comma belongs just before the verb, it might. However, the writer should also go back and look to see where the other comma should go. If the sentence still makes sense, then the pair of commas belongs.

The challenge in punctuating an E Structure sentence is deciding what is necessary (**restrictive**) and what is unnecessary (**nonrestrictive**) information. Unfortunately, it's not as simple as looking for key words, such as subordinating or coordinating conjunctions. Instead, deciding whether information is important or unimportant depends on the meaning of the words in the sentence. The following is a good example:

> My sister Sherry lives in Indiana.
> My sister, Sherry, lives in Indiana.

As subtle as it may seem, the punctuation in these sentences tells the reader how many sisters the writer has. In the first sentence, the writer has several sisters and is making the point that the sister named Sherry lives in Indiana. In the second sentence, the writer has only one sister. The commas are a simple way of saying, "By the way, her name is Sherry." Most of the time, the significance of the commas or lack of commas will not be critical. However, on occasion, meaning can be changed dramatically, as in the following sentences:

> Hank's wife, Agnes, loves to cook.
> Hank's wife Agnes loves to cook.

In the first sentence, Hank has one wife. Her name is Agnes. The second sentence tells us that Agnes is *one* of Hank's wives. The simple placement of commas greatly affects the meaning of these sentences.

The Grammar Notebook   ECS Learning Systems, Inc.

■ Tip

As a general rule, the word *that* introduces restrictive (necessary) information, and the word *which* introduces nonrestrictive (unimportant) information.

In this case, **nonrestrictive** information is separated off with a comma, just as it would be elsewhere in the sentence. In the following sentences, notice how the meaning changes depending on whether the information is considered necessary or unnecessary.

Restrictive (necessary): He gave her the book that had been his grandmother's.
(The book was important because it had been his grandmother's.)

Nonrestrictive (unnecessary): He gave her the book, which had been his grandmother's.
(He gave her a specific book; by the way, it had been his grandmother's.)

It's Your Turn
Sentence Structures A, B, C, D, and E

■ **Practice**

Directions: Identify the following sentences as A, B, C, D, or E Structure sentences. Circle the nonrestrictive (unnecessary) material in the E Structure sentences. Punctuate each sentence correctly.

_____ 1. Writing like life itself is a voyage of discovery. —*Henry Miller*

_____ 2. We know so many things that aren't so. —*Proverb*

_____ 3. It is the lack of confidence more than anything else that kills a civilization.
—*Kenneth Clark*

_____ 4. So often when we say "I love you" we say it with a huge "I" and a small "you."
—*Archbishop Antony*

_____ 5. Wisdom is the reward you get for a lifetime of listening when you'd have preferred to talk. —*Doug Larson*

_____ 6. Trim sentences like trim bodies usually require far more effort than flabby ones.
—*Clair Kehrwald Cook*

_____ 7. If you don't know where you're going any road will take you there. —*Proverb*

_____ 8. Trifles make perfection and perfection is no trifle. —*Michaelangelo*

_____ 9. Nothing has come along that can beat the horse and buggy. —*Chauncy Depew*

_____ 10. Not everything that can be counted on counts and not everything that counts can be counted. —*Albert Einstein*

■ **Write Your Own**

Directions: On a separate sheet of paper, write five E Structure sentences.

> **Examples: (Nonrestrictive)** The cat, who needed therapy, fainted.
> **(Restrictive)** The dog in the tree barked.

ECS Learning Systems, Inc.

Summary Sheet: A, B, C, D, and E Structure Sentences

Sentence Structure A	
Examples	**Features**
The dog barked. The cat fainted.	• one independent clause • no internal punctuation needed

Sentence Structure B	
Examples	**Features**
The dog barked, and the cat fainted. The dog barked: the cat fainted. The dog barked; therefore, the cat fainted.	• two or more independent clauses connected by a comma and a coordinating conjunction (*for, and, nor, but, or, yet, so*) • two or more independent clauses combined into a single sentence by a semicolon, colon, or dash • two or more independent clauses combined by a semicolon, conjunctive adverb or transitional phrase, and a comma

Sentence Structure C	
Example	**Features**
The cat fainted because the dog barked.	• independent clause followed by one or more dependent adverbial clauses • no internal punctuation needed • dependent clause signaled by a subordinating conjunction

Sentence Structure D	
Example	**Features**
After hearing the dog bark, the cat fainted. When the dog barked, the cat fainted.	• dependent adverbial clause, phrase, or word followed by an independent clause • dependent clause generally signaled by a subordinating conjunction • a comma separates the two

Sentence Structure E	
Example	**Features**
The cat, who needed therapy, fainted.	• independent clause with a nonrestrictive (unnecessary) interruption between the subject and predicate • a pair of parentheses, commas, or dashes is used

Not an E Structure Sentence	
Example	**Features**
The dog in the tree barked.	• independent clause with a restrictive (necessary) interruption between the subject and the predicate • no punctuation is used

ECS Learning Systems, Inc.   The Grammar Notebook

It's Your Turn
More Sentence Structures A, B, C, D, and E

■ Practice

Directions: The following sentences are combinations of A, B, C, D, and E Structures sentences. Punctuate each sentence correctly.

1. For every problem there is one solution which is simple neat and wrong. —*H.L. Mencken*

2. In composing as a general rule run your pen through every other word you have written you have no idea what vigor it will give to your style. —*Sydney Smith*

3. In times of change it is the learners who will inherit the earth while the learned will find themselves beautifully equipped for a world that no longer exists.

4. In relation to society and government it may be repeated that new ideas are rare in regard to the latter perhaps no more than two really large and new ideas have been developed in as many millenniums. —*Henry Cabot Lodge*

5. When I was younger I could remember anything whether it happened or not.
   —*Mark Twain*

6. You're telling us that the reason things are so bad is that they are so good and they will get better as soon as they get worse? —*John Sununu*

7. Don't forget folks the less you bet the more you lose when you win.
   —*Stickman at Landmark Casino, Las Vegas*

8. When you reach for the stars you may not quite get one but you won't come up with a handful of mud. —*Leo Burnett*

9. I think most of us are looking for a calling not a job most of us like the assembly line worker have had jobs that are too small for our spirit. —*Nora Watson*

10. When a dog bites a man that is not news but when a man bites a dog that is news.
    —*Charles Anderson Dana*

■ Write Your Own

Directions: On a separate sheet of paper, write your own sentences that combine the different sentence structures.

ECS Learning Systems, Inc.

Review

■ What Have You Learned So Far?

1. Review the summary sheet of the five sentence structures. Notice how, by rearranging the same independent clauses, the importance of each piece of information changes. Look at the following sentences. What observations can you make about subordinating and emphasizing information? Level of formality? Ease of reading?

   a. The dog barked, and the cat fainted.

   b. The dog barked; therefore, the cat fainted.

   c. The dog barked: the cat fainted.

   d. The cat fainted while the dog barked.

   e. When the dog barked, the cat fainted.

   f. When the cat fainted, the dog barked.

   g. The cat, who needed therapy, fainted.

   h. The dog in the tree barked.

2. Review your own writing. Identify the sentence structures you've used. Which sentence structures do you use most often? Why?

3. Which sentence structures would add more clarity or sophistication to your writing?

4. What have you learned about sentence structures so far?

5. Reflect back on your learning process so far. What has been easy to learn? What has been difficult? What in the text helps you to learn? What can you do to improve how you're learning?

   Think about these questions as you answer the following:

   a. What have you learned about clauses, phrases, and sentence structures?

   b. How has this changed your use of language?

   c. What are you still not sure about? How will you gain clarification?

   d. What additional information do you want to learn about clauses, phrases, and sentence structures?

ECS Learning Systems, Inc. The Grammar Notebook

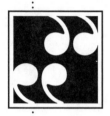 # Tips for Stronger Sentences

Misplaced and Dangling Modifiers

A **modifier** is a word or phrase that describes another word or phrase. Adjectives, adverbs, prepositional phrases, and adjective or adverb clauses are all modifiers. If the modifier is placed at the wrong point in the sentence, the meaning is lost or changed.

Misplaced Modifiers

Misplaced modifiers occur when the modifier is in the wrong place, such as in the following sentences:

> **Confusing:** The boys watched the fire trucks sitting on the roof.
> (Most likely, the boys were on the roof, not the fire trucks.)

> **Clear:** The boys sat on the roof and watched the fire trucks.

> **Confusing:** Flitting around the bird feeder, Neal identified a Western tanager.
> (Was Neal flitting?)

> **Clear:** Neal identified a Western tanager flitting around the bird feeder.

The Grammar Notebook   ECS Learning Systems, Inc.

Dangling Modifiers

A **dangling modifier** occurs when it's not clear who or what the modifier describes. This often happens when the writer begins a phrase with a present or past participle or a gerund (*–ing, –ed*).

> **Confusing:** Leaving a stench throughout the neighborhood, Mark checked for skunks. (Maybe Mark stinks; more likely, the skunks do.)

> **Clear:** Mark checked for skunks, which were leaving a stench throughout the neighborhood.

> **Confusing:** While feeding the chickens, a bull snake slithered into the chicken house. (Was a bull snake feeding the chickens?)

> **Clear:** While I was feeding the chickens, a bull snake slithered into the chicken house.

In these examples, readers can probably make sense of what the writer intended. However, they will probably have to read the sentence at least twice to put the pieces in place. Remember, it's the writer's job to make sure the reader only has to read a sentence once.

■ Discuss

A little carelessness in word choice can dramatically change your intended meaning, as the following two sentences illustrate:

> Everyone was *almost* asleep.

> Almost *everyone* was asleep.

Notice how the meaning in the following sentences changes just by moving the modifier around:

1. *Only* Sheila asked her neighbor to clean up his son's toys yesterday. (None of the other neighbors cared.)

2. Sheila *only* asked her neighbor to clean up his son's toys yesterday. (She asked, but she didn't get down on her knees and beg.)

3. Sheila asked *only* her neighbor to clean up his son's toys yesterday. (She didn't expect anyone else in town to clean up.)

4. Sheila asked her *only* neighbor to clean up his son's toys yesterday. (All of Sheila's other neighbors have moved away because she's such a nag.)

5. Sheila asked her neighbor *only* to clean up his son's toys yesterday. (She didn't ask him to get rid of his son as well, even though that's what she would have preferred.)

6. Sheila asked her neighbor to clean up *only* his son's toys yesterday. (Sheila's own son could leave his toys wherever he liked. Perhaps this is why the other neighbors moved.)

7. Sheila asked her neighbor to clean up his *only* son's toys yesterday. (The neighbor has eleven daughters but only one son. The girls, of course, clean up after themselves.)

8. Sheila asked her neighbor to clean up his son's *only* toys yesterday. (The poor boy only has two toys, and he'd left them both outside.)

9. Sheila asked her neighbor to clean up his son's toys *only* yesterday. (Funny you should mention the toy mess today. Sheila actually talked to the neighbor about it yesterday.)

10. Sheila asked her neighbor to clean up his son's toys yesterday *only*. (The rest of the time it doesn't bother her, but with the President stopping by—well, you get the idea.)

■ Tip

Keep the modifier next to or as close as possible to the word or phrase it describes. Single-word modifiers come directly before the words they modify.

It's Your Turn
Misplaced and Dangling Modifiers

■ Practice

Directions: Underline the dangling or misplaced modifiers in the following sentences. Rewrite each sentence so that the meaning is clearer.

Incorrect: <u>Looking green and fuzzy</u>, I decided to throw away the leftover rice.

Correct: I decided to throw away the leftover rice, which looked green and fuzzy.

1. Sick with worry, the boys finally arrived home.

2. The information was almost appreciated by everyone.

3. Planning to catch the first bus, the waiting room was full of people.

4. The patients were treated by the nurses wearing pajamas.

5. Driving through the countryside, the sun beamed down.

6. Though a young child, the policeman believed the witness.

7. We've tried to teach our children that drinking and driving can be deadly before it's too late.

8. She just drank two cups of coffee and still couldn't sleep.

9. The guard reminded us not to take pictures at the door.

10. While shopping, I sampled a new vegetable dip at the grocery store that tasted like a combination of seaweed and dill.

ECS Learning Systems, Inc.

■ Write Your Own

Dangling Modifiers

Directions: On a separate sheet of paper, combine the two sentences in each pair into a single sentence. Drop all the unnecessary words. Be careful that the modifiers are clear and correctly placed.

1. Ann is growing stronger every day. Her exercise program seems to be working.

2. The cat is climbing to the top branch. My uncle is climbing up to rescue her.

3. The horse is feeling its oats. I'm having trouble riding him.

4. Del's secretary is shying away from taking on more responsibility. Del needs to help manage the secretary's time.

5. Violence in some schools is a problem. Parents often look to those schools for a solution.

6. Amy is unclear about the rules. She has come in late every day for the last week.

7. Bob is tired of waiting for Nan. She's afraid he might leave without her.

8. Maria makes great tips delivering pizza. Her best friend would like to deliver pizzas, too.

9. Ed is tired of doing calculus homework. Ed wants to go to a movie with a friend.

10. The boys drove to California after graduation. They discovered the high price of gas along the way.

       ECS Learning Systems, Inc.

Active and Passive Voice

Study the following sentences. Identify all of the differences you see.

> **Passive voice:** A Ming Dynasty vase was broken by me.
> **Active voice:** I broke the Ming Dynasty vase.

1. What are the differences in the two sentences?

2. Who is the doer of the action in each sentence?

3. Where is the doer identified in each sentence?

4. What is the verb in each sentence?

5. Which sentence is more direct? Why?

6. When would it be appropriate to use the first sentence? The second?

7. Sometimes the doer isn't named in a passive voice sentence. What message does this send?

Good writers use **active voice** sentences as much as possible. As you can see from the examples above, the sentence written in active voice is clearer and more direct. It also requires fewer words. This in general creates stronger sentences.

Some writers choose **passive voice** because they think it sounds formal or because they don't have to identify the doer. There are times when the passive voice is appropriate, such as when the writer doesn't know the doer or the doer doesn't need to be named over and over. As a rule, though, it is preferable to write in the active voice as much as possible.

■ Tip

As often as possible, use the active voice. It has more punch and is more forceful and direct, as shown below:

> **Passive voice (what was said):** Mistakes were made.
> **Active voice (what was meant):** I made mistakes.

Study the following chart to better understand the differences between **active** and **passive voice**.

Active Voice **Example:** Dad spilled the milk.	Doer of the Action *(Dad)*	Receiver of the Action *(milk)*	Verb *(spilled)*	Length	When to Use
	• The subject • Usually named at the beginning of the clause	• The direct object • Follows the verb	• May be any tense • Will always be one word shorter than passive voice	• If the doer is named, will always be shorter than passive voice sentence.	• As much as possible!

Passive Voice **Example:** The milk was spilled by Dad.	Doer of the Action *(by Dad)*	Receiver of the Action *(milk)*	Verb *(was spilled)*	Length	When to Use
	• The object of the preposition (often the word *by*) • Usually named at the end of the clause • May not be named	• The subject • Usually named at the beginning of the clause	• Will always include the present or past participle of *to be* • Will always be one word longer than active voice	• If the doer is not named, may be shorter than active voice sentence.	• When the doer is unimportant or unknown

ECS Learning Systems, Inc.

It's Your Turn
Active and Passive Voice

■ Practice

Directions: Turn the following passive voice sentences into active voice. If it isn't clear who the doer is, make one up.

> **Passive Voice:** Colorado Springs was founded by William Jackson Palmer in 1871.
> **Active Voice:** William Jackson Palmer founded Colorado Springs in 1871.

1. A statue of Palmer was erected in the intersection of Nevada and Platte.

2. Often, accidents are caused by the dangerous placement of the statue.

3. The most frequent accidents are caused by tourists, who have no idea what to do with a statue in the middle of the intersection.

4. Tourists are hit by other tourists as they try to navigate around the roadblock.

5. Every year, the city council is pressured to move the bronze man on horseback to another spot.

6. So far, the attempts have been resisted.

7. But some day, a city council member's car will be hit by a tourist, and the statue will be moved.

8. For now, the statue stays where it is because no one knows where it could be moved.

9. Knowing how these things evolve, the statue will just get moved to a new intersection where more drivers will be inconvenienced by it.

10. So until the city council can determine where more chaos could be caused by the statue, it's left where it is.

■ Write Your Own

Directions: On a separate sheet of paper, write five of your own active voice sentences and five passive voice sentences. Remember that the doer is not always named in a passive voice sentence.

Parallel Sentence Structure

When expressing similar ideas in a sentence, all words, phrases, and clauses should be balanced, or **parallel**, in grammatical structure. Study the italicized words in the following pairs of sentences:

Not parallel: Our remodeling project is finished except for *staining the trim*, *some doors have to be hung*, and *we have to get the carpet installed*.

Parallel: Our remodeling project is finished except for *staining the trim*, *hanging some doors*, and *installing the carpet*.

Not parallel: On weekends, we're either *sailing*, *watch baseball games*, or *we work in the yard*.

Parallel: On weekends, we're either *sailing*, *watching baseball games*, or *working in the yard*.

Not parallel: She finds the new job *stimulating* and a *real challenge*.

Parallel: She finds the new job *stimulating* and *challenging*.

Notice how changing word endings or slightly rearranging words creates a smoother, more seamless effect in the writing. To create parallel structure in sentences containing a pair or series of ideas, use the following guidelines:

1. Balance nouns with nouns and adjectives with adjectives:

    He's an *attentive father*, a *gifted coach*, and a *wise friend*.

2. Use parallel verb tenses:

    As a child, Dusty *loved eating* and *hated waiting*.
    Last week *we waltzed*; this week *we jitterbugged*.

3. Use prepositional phrases in a series:

    We traveled *into the woods* and *out of danger*.

ECS Learning Systems, Inc.

It's Your Turn
Reading for Parallel Sentence Structure

■ Practice

I. **Directions:** The following essay is said to have accompanied an admissions application to Georgetown University. It is an excellent example of parallel construction. Highlight or underline all the examples of parallel structure. Notice how using parallelism contributes to the humor.

I am a dynamic figure, often seen scaling walls and crushing ice. I have been known to remodel train stations on my lunch breaks, making them more efficient in the area of heat retention. I translate ethnic slurs for Cuban refugees. I write award-winning operas. I manage time efficiently. Occasionally, I tread water for three days in a row.

I woo women with my sensuous and godlike trombone playing. I can pilot bicycles up severe inclines with unflagging speed, and I cook thirty-minute brownies in twenty minutes. I am an expert in stucco, a veteran in love, and an outlaw in Peru.

Using only a hoe and a large glass of water, I once single-handedly defended a small village in the Amazon Basin from a horde of ferocious army ants. I play bluegrass cello. I was scouted by the Mets. I am the subject of numerous documentaries. When bored, I build large suspension bridges in my yard. I enjoy urban hang-gliding. On Wednesdays, after school, I repair electrical appliances free of charge.

I am an abstract artist, a concrete analyst, and a ruthless bookie. Critics worldwide swoon over my original line of corduroy evening wear. I don't perspire. I am a private citizen, yet I receive fan mail. I have been Caller Number Nine and won the weekend passes. Last summer I toured New Jersey with a traveling centrifugal-force demonstration. I bat .400. My deft floral arrangements have earned me fame in international botany circles. Children trust me.

ECS Learning Systems, Inc.   The Grammar Notebook

I can hurl tennis rackets at small moving objects with deadly accuracy. I once read *Paradise Lost*, *Moby Dick*, and *David Copperfield* in one day and had time to refurbish an entire dining room that evening. I know the exact location of every item in the supermarket. I have performed several covert operations for the CIA. I sleep once a week; when I do sleep, I sleep in a chair. While on vacation in Canada, I successfully negotiated with a group of terrorists who had seized a small bakery. The laws of physics do not apply to me.

I balance, I weave, I dodge, I frolic, and my bills are all paid. On weekends, to let off steam, I participate in full-contact origami. Years ago, I discovered the meaning of life but forgot to write it down. I have made extraordinary four-course meals using only a mouli and a toaster oven. I breed prize-winning clams. I have won bullfights in San Juan, cliff-diving competitions in Sri Lanka, and spelling bees at the Kremlin. I have played Hamlet, I have performed open-heart surgery, and I have spoken to Elvis.

But I have not yet gone to college.

II. **Directions:** On a separate sheet of paper, rewrite the following sentences using parallel structure.

> **Not parallel:** Every year it takes less time to fly around the world and longer driving to work.

> **Parallel:** Every year it takes less time to fly around the world and more time to drive to work.

1. He would do better in high school if he would study harder, try to sleep some extra hours, and not drink so much soda.

2. She's a great cook, a mediocre housekeeper, and kills anything she plants.

3. Ted's job consists of shuffling papers, then he tells people to get in line, and then to call them over the loudspeaker.

4. Christmas caroling, decorate cookies, and to put up the Christmas tree are all favorite holiday traditions at our house.

5. Today, she won over the town; tomorrow, the state is her goal.

■ Write Your Own

Directions: On a separate sheet of paper, write five of your own sentences using parallel structure.

ECS Learning Systems, Inc.   The Grammar Notebook

Review

■ What Have You Learned So Far?

Reflect on your learning process so far. What has been easy to learn? What has been difficult? What in the text helps you to learn? What can you do to improve how you're learning? Think about these questions as you answer the following:

1. What have you learned about writing stronger sentences?

2. How has this changed your use of language?

3. What are you still not sure about? How will you gain clarification?

4. What additional information do you want to learn about writing stronger sentences?

ECS Learning Systems, Inc.

Appendix

ECS Learning Systems, Inc. The Grammar Notebook

What's Your Learning Style?

Traditionally, most school subjects are taught with the teacher doing all the talking and the students doing all the listening. Some students are able to learn easily this way, but most learn best by using one or a combination of sensory learning styles: **Visual**—watching or reading, **Auditory**—listening, or **Kinesthetic**—touching or doing. Learning efficiency improves when all three styles are used together.

To help determine your own learning style, highlight or underline the following characteristics that describe how you most like to learn.

Visual	Auditory	Kinesthetic
prefer to watch first then do	prefer to have instructions given verbally	prefer to learn by doing
stay focused on the task	easily distracted	like to be in motion
notice detail	enjoy listening to books on tape	use hands while talking
careful about appearance	hum or sigh, often without realizing it	dress for comfort
good speller	poor speller	poor speller
remember faces	sometimes have trouble with written instructions	touch people while talking
quiet by nature	outgoing by nature	outgoing, often very expressive
good handwriting	enjoy talking	like to try new things
organized, like things in neat piles	distracted by noises	like activities
good at puzzles	like rhythm	enjoy dramas
enjoy reading	like to be read to	have low interest in reading
memorize by seeing	memorize by hearing	memorize by doing

The Grammar Notebook ECS Learning Systems, Inc.

Teaching What You Know

One of the most effective ways to learn something is to teach it. Use the following list to plan what and how you'll teach.

1. What concept will you teach? It's not necessary to choose something you understand thoroughly. In fact, for the purpose of this exercise, you may want to choose a concept that you find difficult or confusing. In the process of preparing to teach, you'll be more likely to look at the concept from another perspective and explain it in a new way.

2. To whom will you teach it? What does this person or group already know about this concept? Do they consider it an easy or difficult concept?

3. In what ways is this concept similar to something your audience already knows well?

4. In what ways does the concept fit or break the rules your audience knows?

5. What strategies can you give your audience to help them to learn and remember the concept?

6. How can you combine visual, auditory, and kinesthetic elements into the lesson? How will you reinforce the learning?

The TRUSS System

The key to learning standard grammar is to use it every chance you get. The more you practice it, the more comfortable it will become. The more comfortable it becomes, the more it will sound right to your ear. The more it sounds right, the more automatic making the correct choice will become.

The **T**(hink about function) **R**(earrange) **U**(se) **S**(implify) **S**(ubstitute) system is an excellent way to remember the strategies you can use to make grammatically correct word choices. The following demonstrates using the TRUSS system to work through common problematic pronoun/verb issues.

T(hink about function): What is the **function** of the word you need?

Think about the following sentence:

> The winner is *Tina*.

If *Tina* is replaced with a pronoun, it's helpful to remember that the pronoun will rename *winner*, which makes the pronoun a **subject complement** (or a **predicate nominative**). Consequently, the pronoun must be in the **subjective case**.

> The winner is *she*.

T R(earrange): Turn questions into statements; flip-flop subject complements and subjects to test; rearrange sentences that begin with *there is* or *there are* to find the subject. Whenever possible, manipulate sentences into a more familiar pattern.

> The winner is *she/her*.
> *She/~~her~~* is the winner.
>
> What **is/are** the answer to number three and four?
> The answer to number three and four *~~is~~/are* what?
>
> There **is/are** many people in Chicago.
> Many people *~~is~~/are* in Chicago.
>
> The parents **is/are** they.
> They *~~is~~/are* the parents.

ECS Learning Systems, Inc.

T R U(se): The best way to learn standard grammar is to use it every chance you write or speak. Be aware of how others use language. Who consistently uses standard grammar? Consciously imitate their usage until it becomes more natural for you.

T R U S(implify): Take out prepositional phrases or compound elements. Simplify the sentence down to the bare essentials.

A dinner of steak and potatoes *was/were* prepared by Lisa and *me/I*.

A dinner ~~of steak and potatoes~~ *was/were* prepared by ~~Lisa and~~ *me/I*.

A dinner of steak and potatoes was prepared by Lisa and me.

T R U S S(ubstitute): Most of the time, you know an example or many examples of the standard form of a grammatical rule. Whenever you're not sure of the standard form, substitute an example of what you are sure about.

To *who/whom* should I give the money?

Should I give the money to *who/whom*?

Should I give the money to *him*?

Him and *whom* are both objective case pronouns. *Whom* is the correct answer.

ECS Learning Systems, Inc.   The Grammar Notebook

The Gunning Fog Index

The Gunning Fog Index is one way to determine the reading level of what you've written. This is only one of many formulas that measure readability, but it's a fairly simple one. In addition, many computer word processing programs have readability indexes as part of the software. While it's valuable to know at what grade level you're writing, be aware that all of these tools may simply count the number of words or syllables in a sentence or paragraph or use a list of vocabulary words to gauge difficulty.

No index can truly measure the complexity of ideas. Simple ideas can be written at an advanced level, and complicated ideas can—if the writer is very skillful—be written at an elementary-school level. Most readers, even highly-skilled ones, would prefer to read clear ideas on a simpler level than to concentrate and wade through long, jargon-filled sentences. Keep in mind what you would prefer as a reader!

■ Practice

I. **Directions:** Use the following process to determine the reading level of a passage.

1. Select several 100-word passages from the material. Choose from the beginning, middle, and end of the material.

2. Determine the average number of words in a sentence by counting the number of sentences in each 100-word sample and dividing 100 by the number of sentences.

3. Count the number of words with three or more syllables. Do not count proper names, easy compound words such as *grandmother*, or forms in which the third syllable is merely an ending such as *directed*.

4. Add the number of "hard" words (three syllables or more) to the average number of words in the sentence. Next, multiply this total by 0.4, which is the Gunning Fog "Index." Round off this number to get an approximate grade level for the material.

ECS Learning Systems, Inc.

Example: Use the following sample paragraph to practice determining reading level.

> Education and baseball—analogies abound. Think for a few minutes of teachers and students in a traditional classroom situation as the pitcher and catcher on a baseball team. They're both on the same team and have common goals. The pitcher's purpose is to throw the ball; the catcher's is to catch. As the ball flies through the air, somewhere between the pitcher and the catcher, the responsibility shifts. The catcher is not responsible for the ball while it's still in the pitcher's hands, and the pitcher—even when the ball is poorly thrown—is not responsible for the ball once it reaches the catcher's vicinity. So it is in the traditional classroom. The teacher delivers information and students receive it. Once the teacher has "pitched" the information, it's up to the student to "catch" it. Somewhere in the process, the responsibility shifts from the teacher to the student. Even if the information is poorly taught, the student is expected to know it.

1. Count the first 100 words in this passage. Ignore the rest of the paragraph. (The 100th word is the word *once* in the sixth sentence.)

2. Count the number of sentences in the first 100 words. (5.9)

3. Divide 100 by 5.9. This will give you the average number of words in a sentence. (16.9)

4. Count the number of words of three syllables or more. (7 words: *education, analogies, traditional, situation, responsibility, responsible, responsible*)

5. Add the average number of words in a sentence and the number of "hard" words: 16.9 + 7 = 23.9

6. Multiply the sum by the Gunning Fog Index: 23.9 x 0.4 = 9.6

Result: The reading level is ninth grade, sixth month.

ECS Learning Systems, Inc.

II. **Directions:** Return to the examples of writing that you examined in the previous exercise. Determine the reading level of each.

1. Is the reading level appropriate for the intended audience? For instance, is a ninth-grade science book written at the ninth-grade level (or lower), or is it written at the twelfth-grade level (or higher)?

2. What could the writer do to change the reading level to a more appropriate grade level?

3. How would this impact the quality of writing? The style?

4. How does the level of writing impact the ability to understand the content?

III. **Directions:** Examine your own writing.

1. Is the reading level appropriate for the intended audience?

2. What could you do to change the reading level to a more appropriate grade level?

3. How would this impact the quality of your writing? the style?

4. How would this impact the clarity of the content?

ECS Learning Systems, Inc.

More Tips for Stronger Sentences

Consider the Reader

Central to becoming a good writer is the awareness that all writing will eventually be read by someone. Jacqueline Berke points out the obvious when she states, "All writing is done for human beings by human beings." Yet writers so often seem to forget that readers can be easily distracted or may not care about the subject enough to wade through jargon or fuzzy sentences.

Many novice writers make the mistake of thinking that even if they don't explain an idea clearly a good reader will be able to figure it out anyway. The irony, of course, is that if the writer doesn't care enough to state his or her ideas clearly, why would the reader ever care to decipher them?

Skilled writers know the secret to good writing is this: *Don't make the reader work.* This ability requires attention to many elements, including the following:

- identifying the audience

- writing for the appropriate reading level

- shifting the tone and style to match the reader

- avoiding inflated words and phrases

- using lively images

- keeping information clear and simple

As writers understand the idea of writing for the reader, words come more easily and ideas flow more smoothly. To accomplish this, they can ask themselves the following questions about their own writing:

- Why would I read this?

- What do I want to learn from it?

- How should this be organized so the information will be clearer?

- What transition words or phrases would make the ideas easier to follow?

- What devices would help hold my attention longer?

Avoid Opinion Phrases

Examine the following pairs of writing samples:

Norman Cousins:

A. I think professional athletes are sometimes severely disadvantaged by trainers whose job it is to keep them in action.

B. Professional athletes are sometimes severely disadvantaged by trainers whose job it is to keep them in action.

Rockwell Stenrud:

A. In my opinion, there are seven basic signals that get communicated from the [baseball] manager… to the players.

B. In general, there are seven basic signals that get communicated from the [baseball] manager… to the players.

Adam Smith:

A. Nicotine is a familiar and widely recognized drug, a stimulant to the central nervous system. I believe it is addictive.

B. Nicotine is a familiar and widely recognized drug, a stimulant to the central nervous system. It is addictive.

Willard Gaylin:

A. A New York taxi driver… is licensed to operate, and thereby earn his living, by the city. One of the rules in the taxi code stipulates that the cabdriver must take his customer to any point within the city limits that the rider requests. Never mind that the driver makes more money operating in Manhattan; is lost when he enters the precincts of Brooklyn; is frightened by the prospect of a trip to Harlem at night. I think the rules are clear. He must go where the customer asks.

B. A New York taxi driver… is licensed to operate, and thereby earn his living, by the city. One of the rules in the taxi code stipulates that the cabdriver must take his customer to any point within the city limits that the rider requests. Never mind that the driver makes more money operating in Manhattan; is lost when he enters the precincts of Brooklyn; is frightened by the prospect of a trip to Harlem at night. The rules are clear. He must go where the customer asks.

ECS Learning Systems, Inc.

1. Which statement in each pair is stronger? More convincing?

2. What makes the difference?

3. How do opinion phrases strengthen or weaken the message?

4. Are they ever appropriate—even important—to use?

Examine your own work to find opinion phrases. Delete the phrases or change them to more forceful direct statements.

Examine Others' Writing

The best writers study the writing of others. They observe how others craft sentences, create descriptions, and organize information. What can you learn from how others write?

Select writing examples from a variety of writers and sources. Include examples such as a newspaper, a textbook, an encyclopedia, a novel, and a magazine.

1. What do you like or not like about the example?

2. What makes each writer different from the others?

3. Which ones are easy to read? Why?

4. Which ones are hard to read? Why?

5. How does sentence length and word choice impact the ease of reading?

ECS Learning Systems, Inc.

New Word List

Word_____

How you learned it

_____

_____

_____

How and when you used it

_____

_____

_____

Word_____

How you learned it

_____

_____

_____

How and when you used it

_____

_____

_____

The Grammar Notebook   ECS Learning Systems, Inc.

Usage Errors

Error

_____

_____

_____

_____

What the correct usage should be

_____

_____

_____

_____

Was the error intentional? _____

What impact does the error have on the reader or listener?

_____

_____

_____

_____

Answer Key

5   Simple Subjects and Complete Subjects

1. (Time) is the most valuable thing a man can spend.
2. ((You)) Beware the fury of a patient man.
3. Every (society) honors its live conformists and its dead troublemakers.
4. There was never **a great** (genius) without a tincture of madness.
5. Why did **the** (chicken) cross the road?

7   Complete Subjects and Complete Predicates

1. Boundaries (create freedom.)
2. Life and business (are like the car pool lane.) The best way to reach your destination quickly (is to take some people with you.)
3. (You) (take risks.) You (can't fall off the bottom.)
4. People who never get carried away (should be.)
5. _USA Today_ (has come out with a new survey.) Apparently, three out of every four people (make up 75% of the population.)
6. The mind (is an iceberg.) It (floats with only one-seventh of its bulk above water.)
7. The torments of martyrdom (are probably most keenly felt by the bystanders.)
8. Leadership in today's world (requires far more than a large stock of gunboats and a hard fist at the conference table.)
9. Skepticism (is the beginning of faith.)
10. An hour on the lake (is like a day in the city.)

12   Subject/Verb Agreement

1. The committee _are_/(is) planning to celebrate its success. (collective noun functions as a single body)
2. Who _is_/(are) the winners of the Nobel Prize this year? (verb comes before subject)

3. There (*is*)/*are* no such thing as a minor lapse of integrity. (verb comes before subject)

4. Approximately 40 percent of all American households *has*/(*have*) a computer. (subject separated from verb)

5. Either the office staff or Pat (*closes*)/*close* up every night. (closest subject to verb determines whether singular or plural)

6. The perception of the Soviets that has developed over the past 50 years (*is*)/*are* difficult to change. (subject separated from verb)

7. Neither mumps nor measles (*is*)/*are* usually lethal. (words with plural form preceded by *either/or* or *neither/or* take singular verb)

8. The jury (*is*)/*are* arguing heatedly over the defendant's guilt or innocence. (collective noun functioning as a single unit)

9. Mathematics (*is*)/*are* challenging. (words with plural form take singular verb)

10. The people I know who are the most generous *is*/(*are*) the ones who have the least. (subject separated from verb)

18 Clauses

1. ⟨What gets measured⟩ becomes important.
   noun

2. The value of an employee is not in ⟨what he can do⟩ but
   noun

   ⟨what he is willing to do⟩.
   noun

3. It's easier for people to see it your way ⟨if you first see it their way.⟩
   adverb

4. Some succeed ⟨because they are destined to;⟩ most succeed
   adverb
   ⟨because they are determined to.⟩
   adverb

5. A college education seldom hurts a man
   ⟨if he's willing to learn a little something⟩ ⟨after he graduates.⟩
   adverb   **adverb**

6. I had a monumental idea this morning, but I didn't like it.

7. The secret of managing is to keep the guys ⟨who hate you⟩
                                               adjective
   away from the guys ⟨who are undecided.⟩
                      adjective

8. If you're too busy to help those around you succeed, you're too busy.
   adverb

9. How we get to *where we don't know* *we're going* determines
   noun **noun**
   where we end up.
   noun

10. It's not *what you tell them that counts.* It's *what they take away.*
    noun **noun**

20 Sentence Fragments

Answers will vary.

23 Phrases

1. Beware <u>of Greeks</u> <u>bearing gifts</u>.
   prepositional/participle

2. Mother always said <u>to treat others</u> <u>in the way</u> we wanted <u>to be treated</u>.
   infinitive **prepositional** **infinitive**

3. Lisa's favorite pastime is <u>surfing the Internet</u>.
   gerund

4. <u>Sleeping under the table</u>, the kittens seemed content.
   participle

5. She spends most <u>of the morning</u> <u>at her office</u>.
   prepositional **prepositional**

6. <u>For example</u>, Tom is planning <u>to paint the house</u>.
   prepositional **infinitive**

7. <u>Considering the odds</u>, we were surprised <u>to win the lottery</u> twice <u>in a year</u>.
   participle **infinitive** **prepositional**

8. Simple, clear purpose and principles give rise
   <u>to complex and intelligent behavior</u>. Complex rules and regulations give rise
   prepositional
   <u>to simple and stupid behavior</u>.
   prepositional

9. Explorers have <u>to be ready</u> <u>to die lost</u>.
   infinitive phrases

10. <u>In the end</u>, it is attention <u>to detail</u> that makes all the difference.
    prepositional **prepositional**

ECS Learning Systems, Inc.

28   Sentence Structure A

A	1.	A fool and his money are soon partying.
	2.	If you think education is expensive, try ignorance.
A	3.	Visualize whirled peas.
A	4.	Don't believe everything you think.
	5.	When all is said and done, more is said than done.
A	6.	The only way to have a friend is to be one.
A	7.	Eighty percent of success is showing up.
A	8.	Nobody who has not been in the interior of a family can say what the difficulties of any individual of that family may be.
	9.	When you come to a fork in the road, take it.
A	10.	A fanatic is one who can't change his mind and won't change the subject.

33   Sentence Structures A and B

A	1.	Familiarity breeds contempt.
A	2.	Everything that irritates us about others can lead us to an understanding of ourselves.
B	3.	Choose your life's mate carefully; from this one decision will come ninety percent of all your happiness or misery.
A	4.	To love and to be loved is to feel the sun from both sides.
B	5.	It is not easy to find happiness in ourselves, and it is not possible to find it elsewhere.
A	6.	The basic purpose of a liberal arts education is to liberate the human being to exercise his or her potential to the fullest.
B	7.	No man sees far; most see no farther than their noses.
B	8.	Chance is a word void of sense; nothing can exist without a cause.
B	9.	What we anticipate seldom occurs; what we least expect generally happens.
B	10.	Regret is an appalling waste of energy; you can't build on it; it is good only for wallowing in.

37   Sentence Structures A, B, and C

C	1.	Can anybody remember when times were not hard and money not scarce?
C	2.	Problems can become opportunities when the right people come together.
A	3.	Very little is needed to make a happy life.
B	4.	Seize the day; put no trust in the morrow.
C	5.	Our duty is to proceed as if limits to our ability do not exist.

ECS Learning Systems, Inc.   The Grammar Notebook

C	6.	You can outdo you if you really want to.
A	7.	There is no traffic jam on the extra mile.
B	8.	One person can make a difference, and every person should try.
C	9.	We must learn to lift as we climb.
C	10.	There are no exceptions to the rule that everybody likes to be an exception to the rule.

40 Sentence Structures A, B, C, and D

D	1.	If fifty million people say a foolish thing, it is still a foolish thing.
C	2.	Too many people think they are being creative when they are just being different.
D	3.	To me, old age is always fifteen years older than I am.
D	4.	Making the decision to have a child—it's momentous.
D	5.	Toto, we're not in Kansas anymore.
C	6.	The latter part of a wise man's life is taken up in curing the follies, prejudices, and false opinions he contracted in the former.
D	7.	Where all think alike, no one thinks very much.
D	8.	If he works for you, you work for him.
B	9.	Debate is masculine; conversation is feminine.
A	10.	Cauliflower is nothing but cabbage with a college education.

44 Sentence Structures A, B, C, D, and E

E	1.	Writing, like life itself, is a voyage of discovery.
C	2.	We know so many things that aren't so.
E	3.	It is the lack of confidence, more than anything else, that kills a civilization.
D	4.	So often, when we say, "I love you," we say it with a huge "I" and a small "you."
C	5.	Wisdom is the reward you get for a lifetime of listening when you'd have preferred to talk.
E	6.	Trim sentences, like trim bodies, usually require far more effort than flabby ones.
D	7.	If you don't know where you're going, any road will take you there.
B	8.	Trifles make perfection, and perfection is no trifle.
C	9.	Nothing has come along that can beat the horse and buggy.
B	10.	Not everything that can be counted counts, and not everything that counts can be counted.

46   More Sentence Structures A, B, C, D, and E

(Answers may vary.)

1. For every problem there is one solution, which is simple, neat, and wrong.
2. In composing, as a general rule, run your pen through every other word you have written. You have no idea what vigor it will give to your style.
3. In times of change, it is the learners who will inherit the earth while the learned will find themselves beautifully equipped for a world that no longer exists.
4. In relation to society and government, it may be repeated that new ideas are rare. In regard to the latter, perhaps no more than two really large and new ideas have been developed in as many millenniums.
5. When I was younger, I could remember anything, whether it happened or not.
6. You're telling us that the reason things are so bad is that they are so good, and they will get better as soon as they get worse?
7. Don't forget folks, the less you bet, the more you lose when you win.
8. When you reach for the stars, you may not quite get one, but you won't come up with a handful of mud.
9. I think most of us are looking for a calling not a job; most of us, like the assembly line worker, have had jobs that are too small for our spirit.
10. When a dog bites a man, that is not news; but when a man bites a dog, that is news.

51   Misplaced or Dangling Modifiers

(Answers may vary.)

1. I was sick with worry, but the boys finally arrived home.
2. The information was appreciated by almost everyone.
3. The waiting room was full of people planning to catch the first bus.
4. The patients, wearing pajamas, were treated by the nurses.
5. While I was driving through the countryside, the sun beamed down.
6. Though the witness was just a young child, the policeman believed her.
7. We've tried to teach our children before it's too late that drinking and driving can be deadly.
8. She drank just two cups of coffee and still couldn't sleep.
9. The guard reminded us at the door not to take pictures.
10. While shopping at the grocery store, I sampled a new vegetable dip that tasted like a combination of seaweed and dill.

    ECS Learning Systems, Inc.   The Grammar Notebook

55   Active and Passive Voice
(Answers may vary.)

1. The city erected a statue of Palmer in the intersection of Nevada and Platte.
2. Often, the dangerous placement of the statue causes accidents.
3. Tourists, who have no idea what to do with a statue in the middle of the intersection, cause the most frequent accidents.
4. Tourists hit other tourists as they try to navigate around the roadblock.
5. Every year, citizens pressure the city council to move the bronze man on horseback to another spot.
6. So far, the council has resisted the attempts.
7. But some day, a tourist will hit a city council member's car, and the council will move the statue.
8. For now, the statue stays where it is because no one knows where to move it.
9. Knowing how these things evolve, the council will just move the statue to a new intersection where it will inconvenience more drivers.
10. So until the city council can determine where the statue can cause more chaos, it will remain where it is.

57   Reading for Parallel Sentence Structure
(Parallel construction in italics)

I.   I am a dynamic figure, often seen *scaling walls* and *crushing ice*. I have been known to remodel train stations on my lunch breaks, making them more efficient in the area of heat retention. *I translate ethnic slurs for Cuban refugees*. *I write award-winning operas*. *I manage time efficiently*. Occasionally, *I tread water for three days in a row*.

I woo women with my sensuous and godlike trombone playing. I can pilot bicycles up severe inclines with unflagging speed, and I cook thirty-minute brownies in twenty minutes. I am *an expert in stucco*, *a veteran in love*, and *an outlaw in Peru*.

Using only *a hoe* and *a large glass of water*, I once single-handedly defended a small village in the Amazon Basin from a horde of ferocious army ants. I play bluegrass cello. I was scouted by the Mets. *I am* the subject of numerous documentaries. When bored, *I build* large suspension bridges in my yard. *I enjoy* urban hang gliding. On Wednesdays, after school, *I repair* electrical appliances free of charge.

I am *an abstract artist*, *a concrete analyst*, and *a ruthless bookie*. Critics worldwide swoon over my original line of corduroy evening wear. I don't perspire. *I am a private citizen*, yet I *receive fan mail*. I have been Caller Number Nine and won the weekend passes. Last summer I toured New Jersey with a traveling centrifugal-force demonstration. I bat .400. My deft floral arrangements have earned me fame in international botany circles. Children trust me.

I can hurl tennis rackets at small moving objects with deadly accuracy. I once read *Paradise Lost, Moby Dick,* and *David Copperfield* in one day and had time to refurbish an entire dining room that evening. I know the exact location of every item in the supermarket. I have performed several covert operations for the CIA. I sleep once a week; when I do sleep, I sleep in a chair. While on vacation in Canada, I successfully negotiated with a group of terrorists who had seized a small bakery. The laws of physics do not apply to me.

I balance, I weave, I dodge, I frolic, and my bills are all paid. On weekends, to let off steam, I participate in full-contact origami. Years ago, *I discovered the meaning of life* but *forgot to write it down*. I have made extraordinary four-course meals using only a mouli and a toaster oven. I breed prize-winning clams. I have won *bullfights in San Juan, cliff-diving competitions in Sri Lanka,* and *spelling bees at the Kremlin*. *I have played* Hamlet, *I have performed* open-heart surgery, and *I have spoken* to Elvis.

But I have not yet gone to college.

II.   (Answers may vary.)

1. He would do better at college if he would study harder, sleep more, and drink less soda.
2. She's a great cook, a mediocre housekeeper, and a lousy gardener.
3. Ted's job consists of shuffling papers, telling people to get in line, and calling them over the loudspeaker.
4. Christmas caroling, decorating cookies, and putting up the Christmas tree are all favorite holiday traditions at our house.
5. Today, she won over the town; tomorrow, she'll aim for the state.

Notes

The Grammar Notebook   ECS Learning Systems, Inc.